Yacob & Tomás

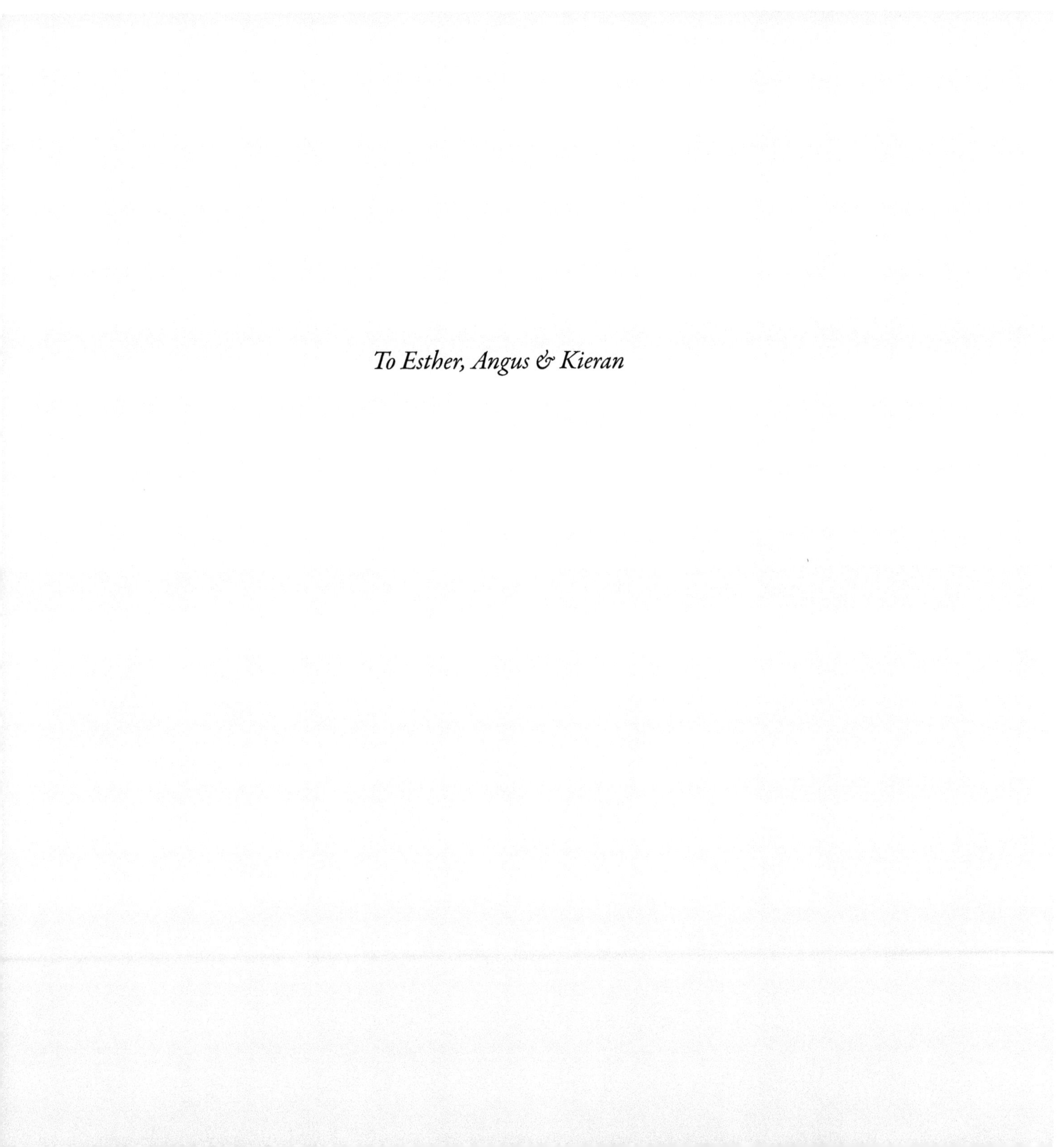

To Esther, Angus & Kieran

Just who is Harris ?

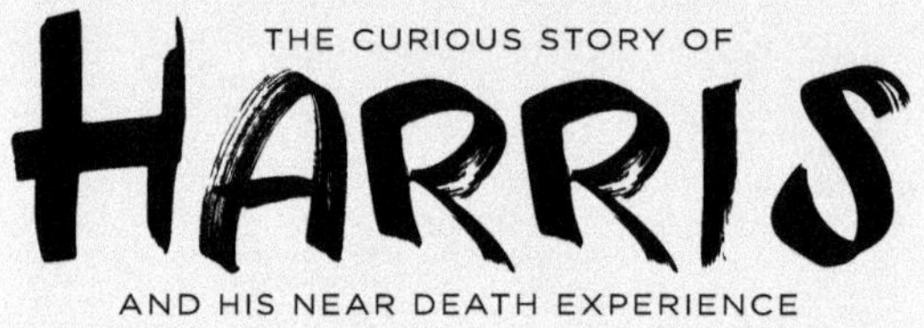

HARRIS

AND HIS NEAR DEATH EXPERIENCE

Information / Media:

Yacob & Tomás
tbgilman@gmail.com

ISBN 978-0-9970008-5-6

Published in the United States of America

Cover Illustration - Nicholas Williamson
Artwork Photography - Angus McNaughton
Book Design - timmyroland.com

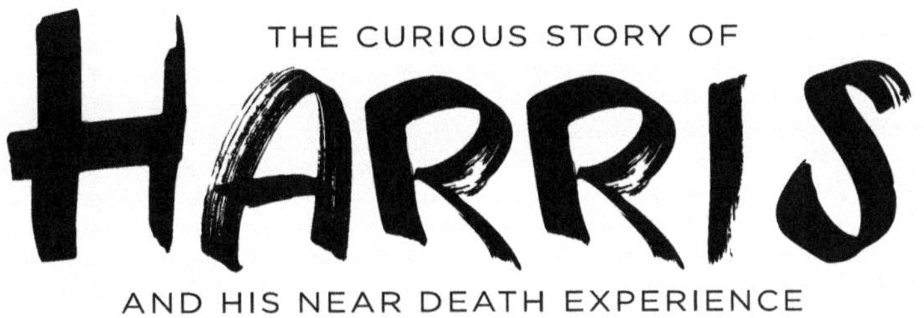

NICHOLAS **WILLIAMSON**

Yacob & Tomás

WORLDWIDE

Harris is not happy.

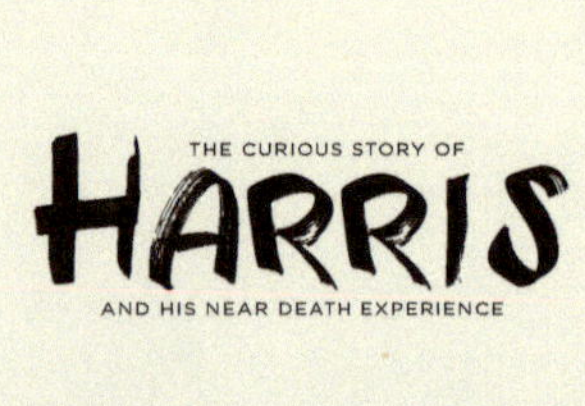

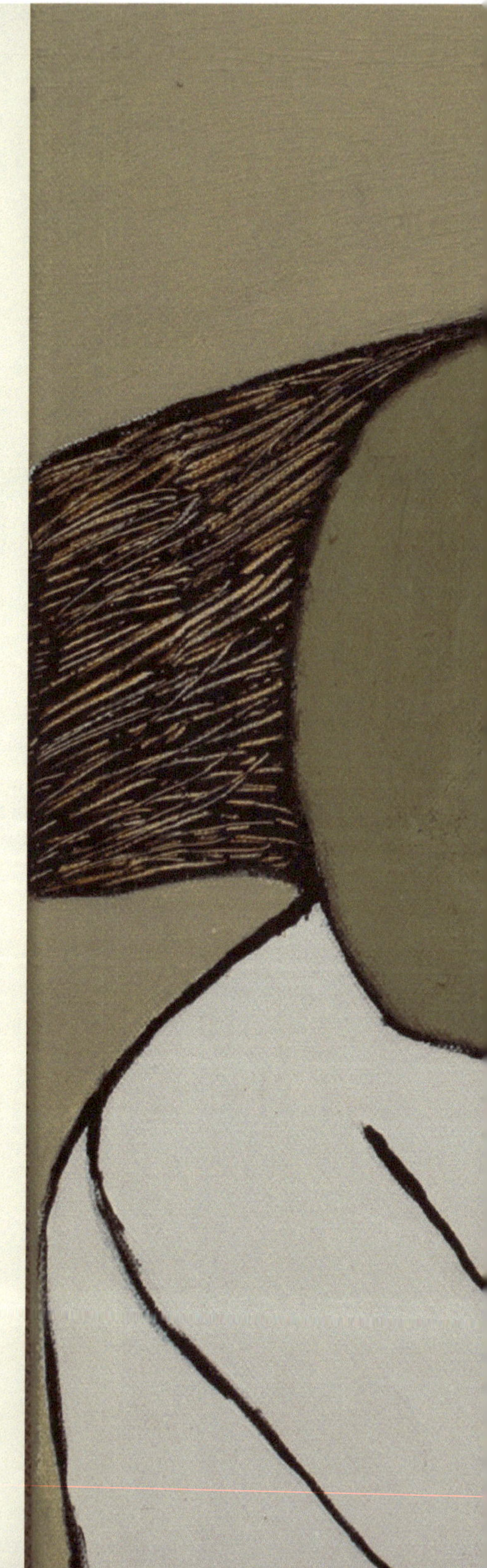

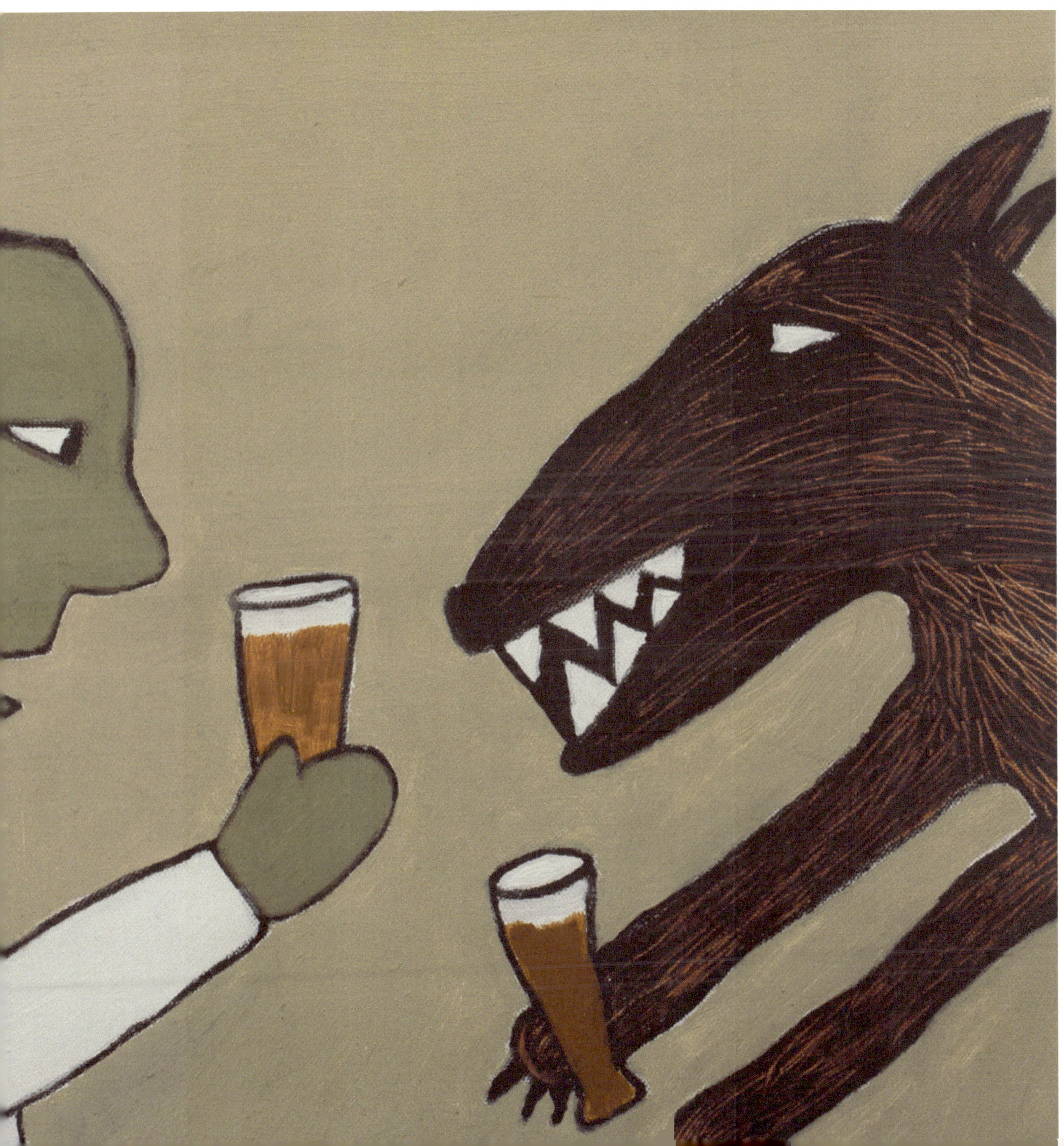

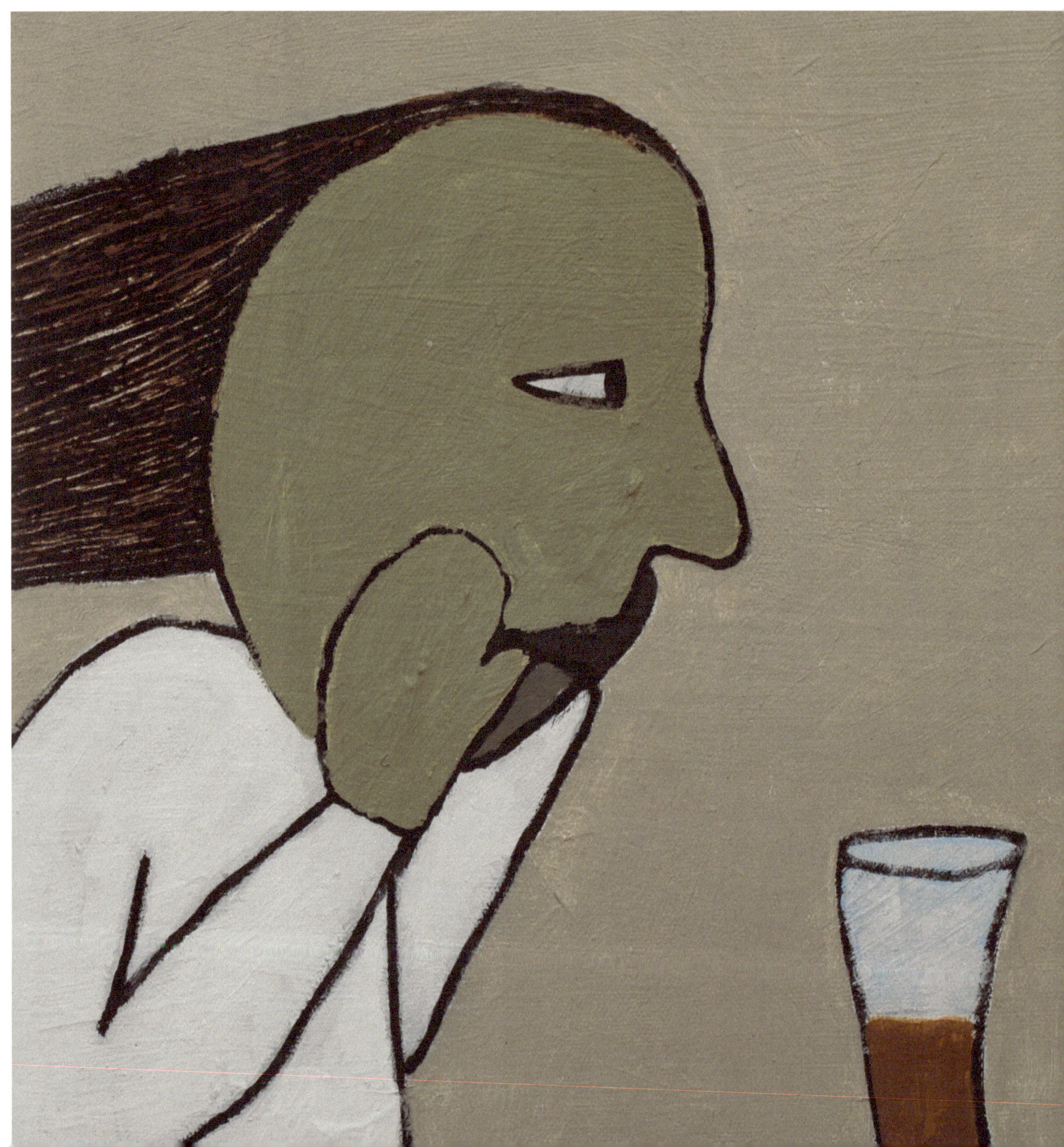

He feels something is missing.

He is surrounded by wolves.

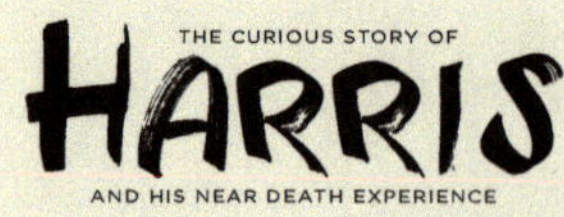

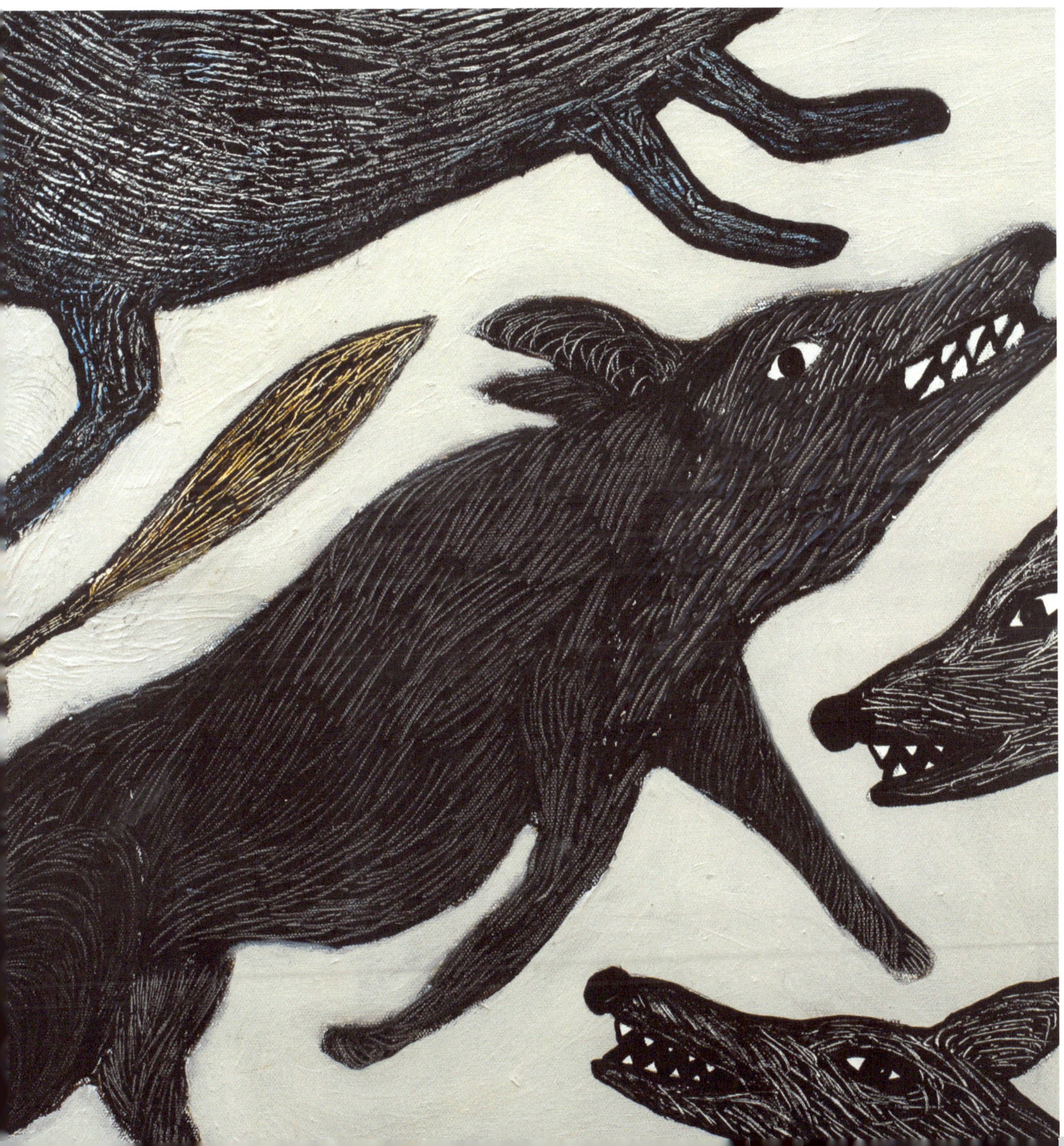

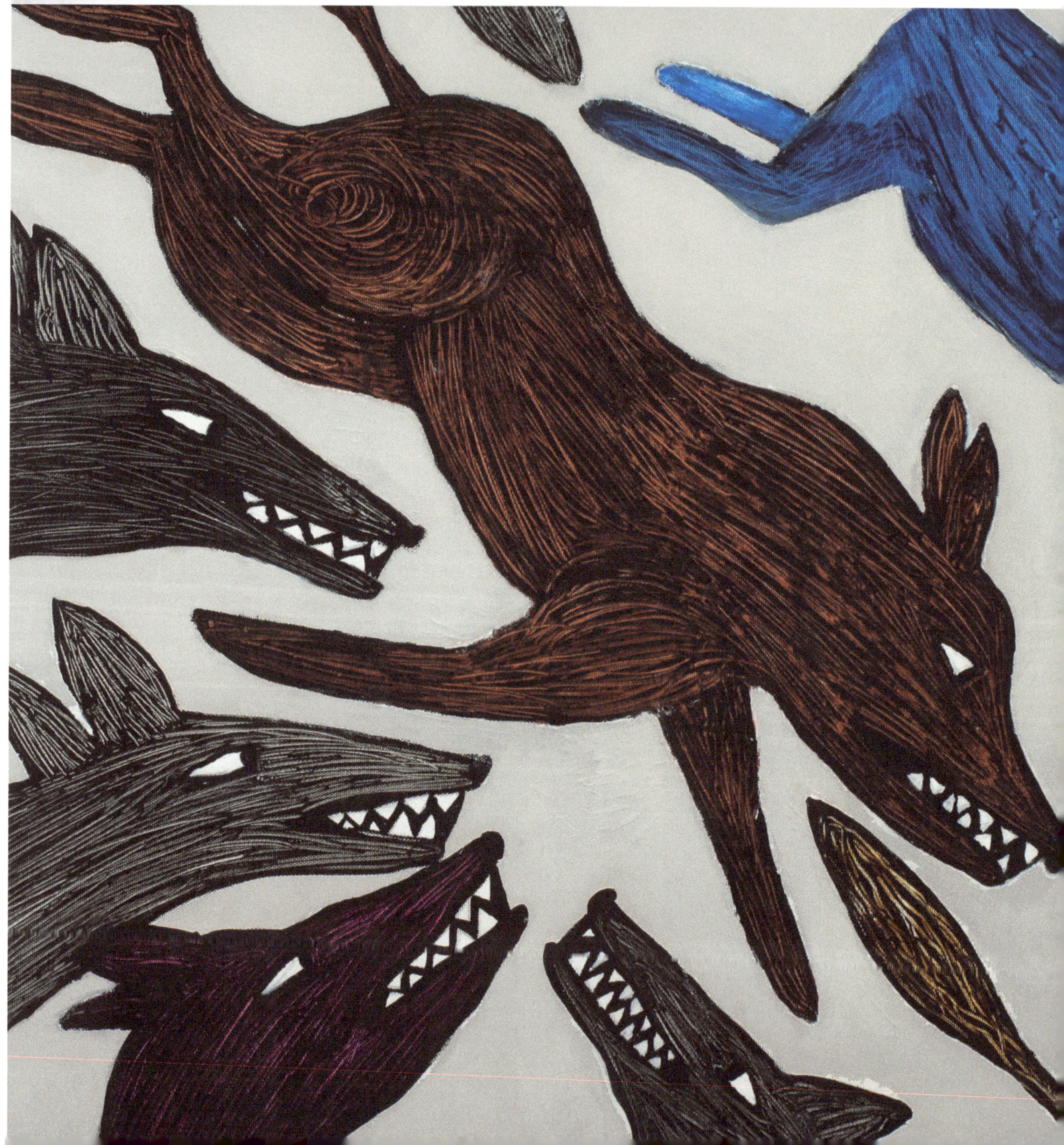

They get inside his head.

Harris looks for the answer.

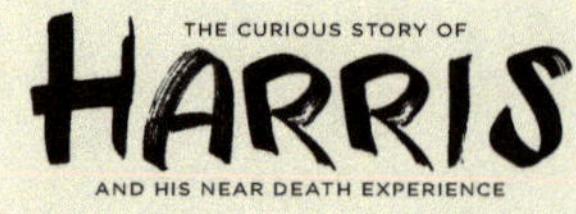

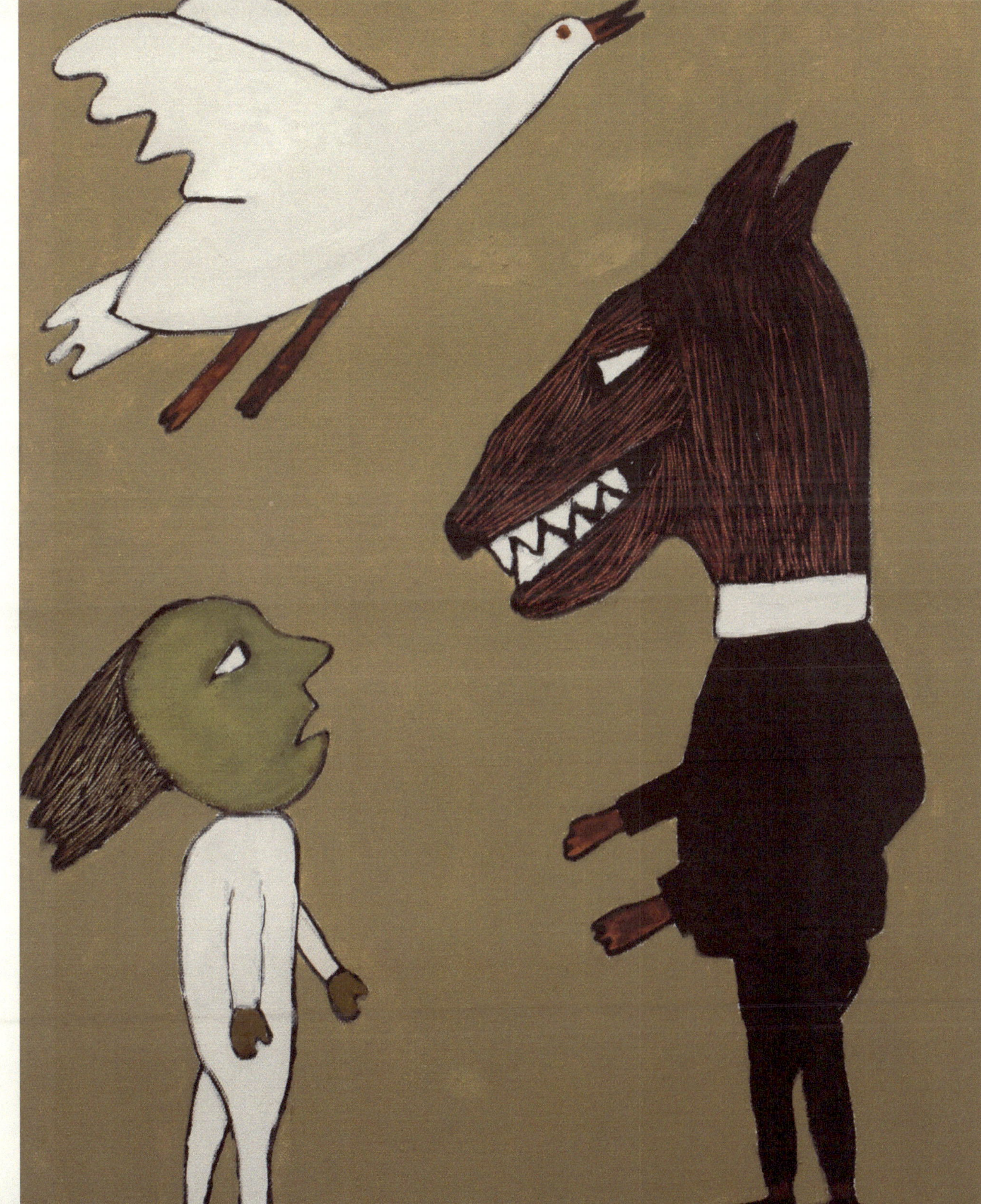

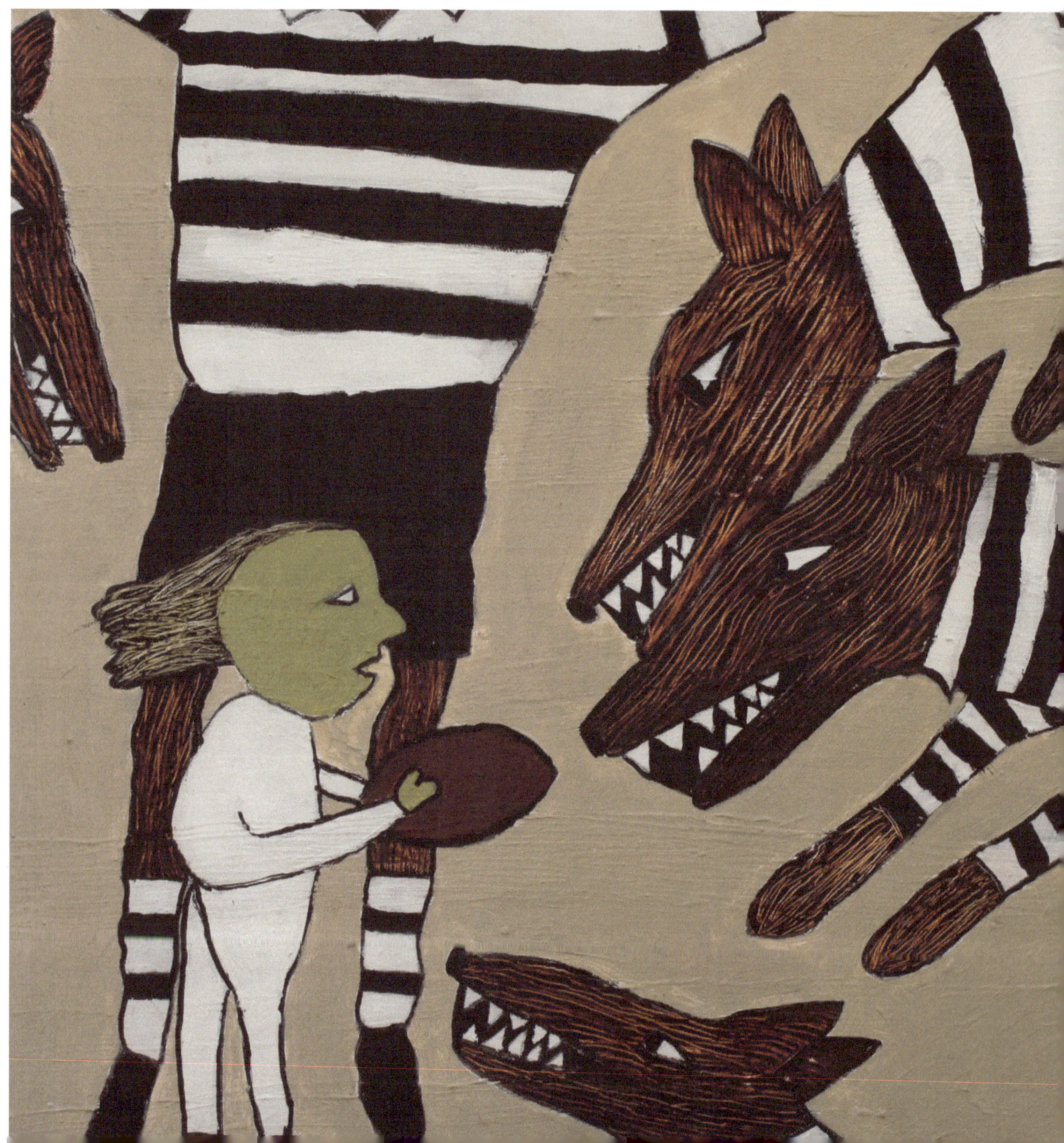

His minister says he should take up rugby . . .

19

. . . or basketball.

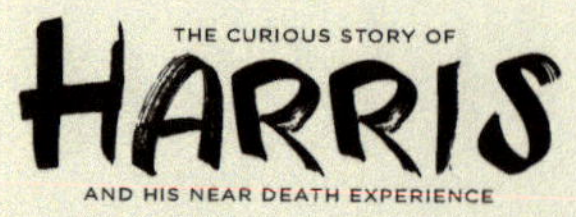

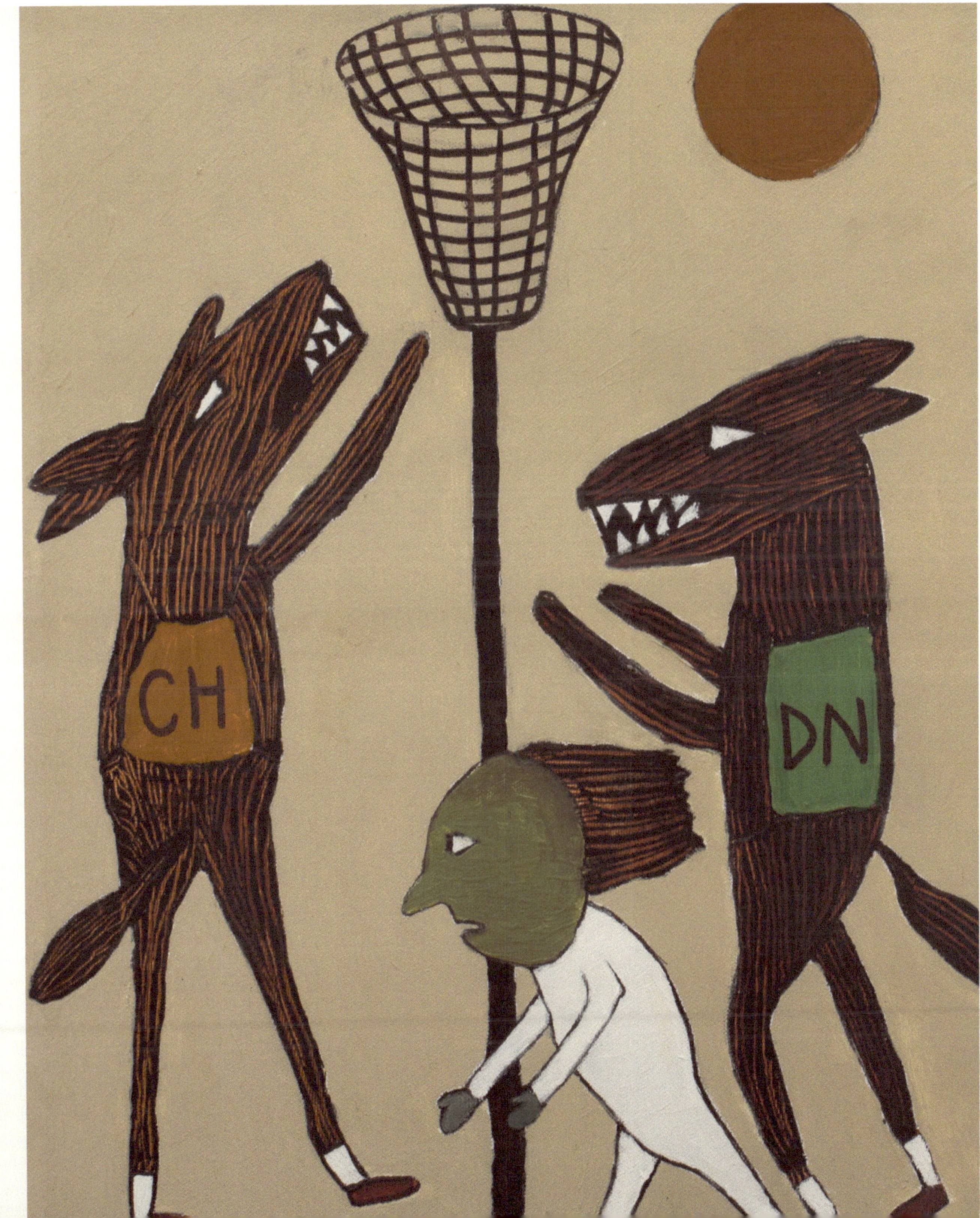

CH
DN

Harris visits a psychiatrist, Dr Birdstein.

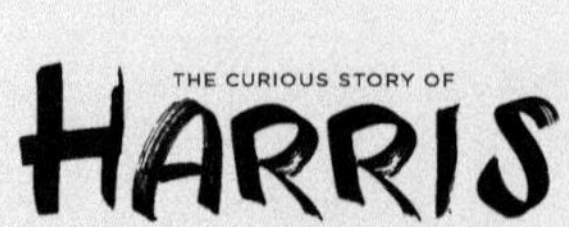

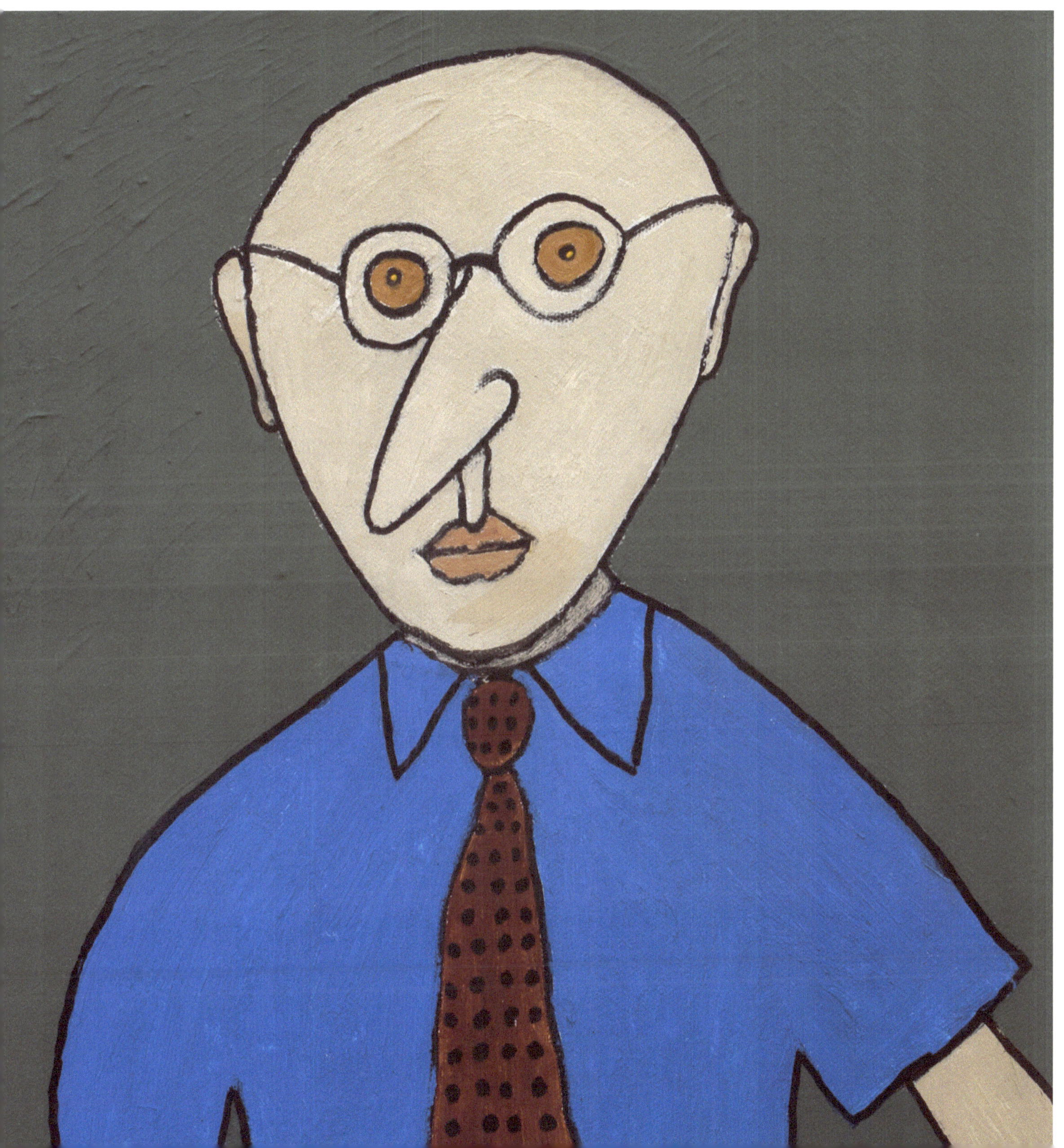

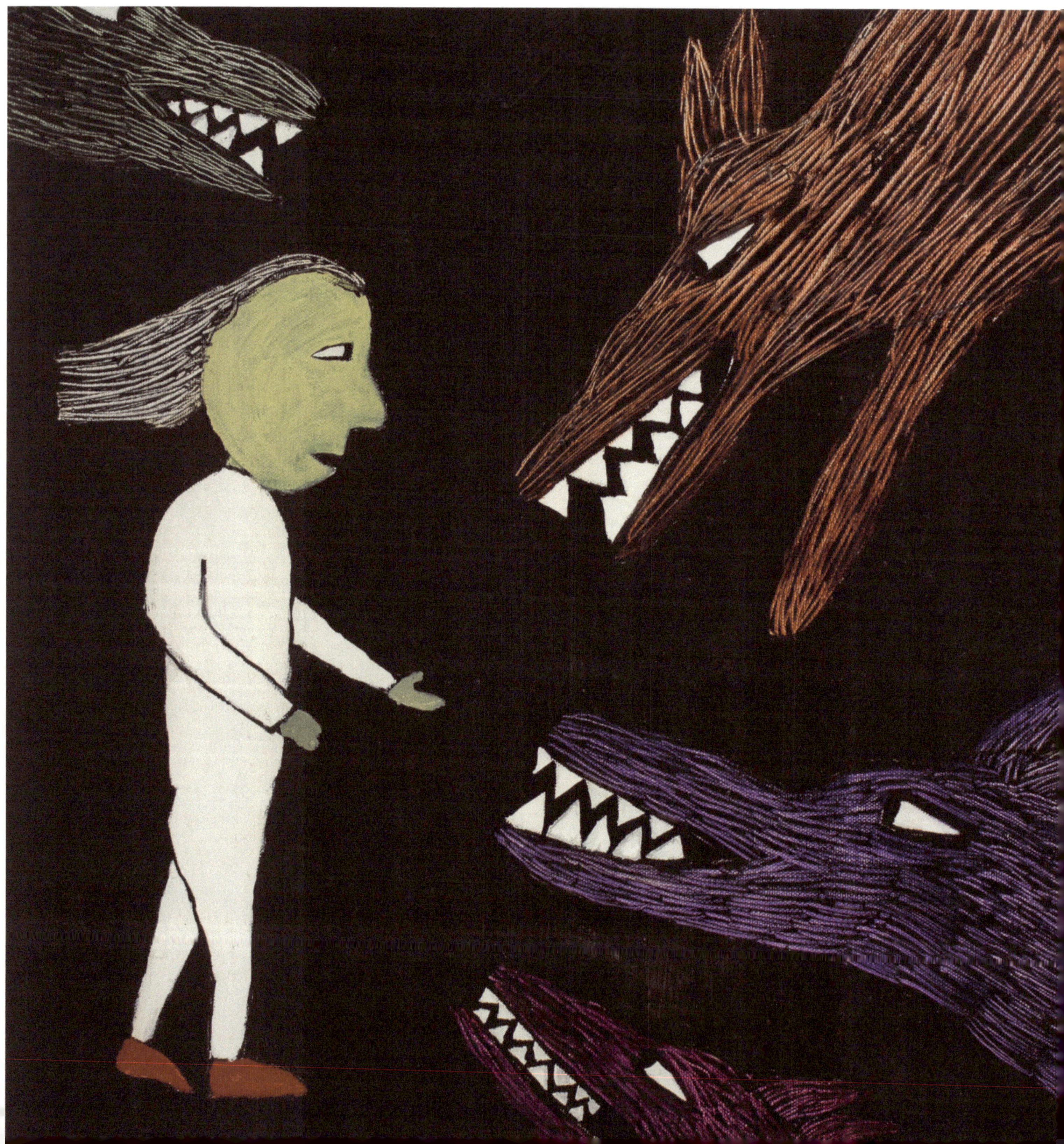

Dr. Birdstein says that Harris must face his demons . . .

. . . and offer his heart to the wolves.

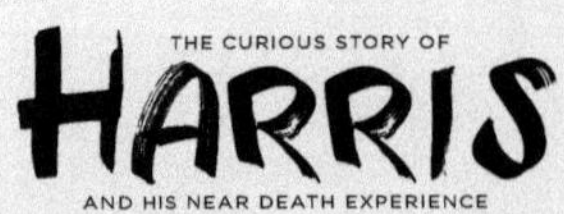

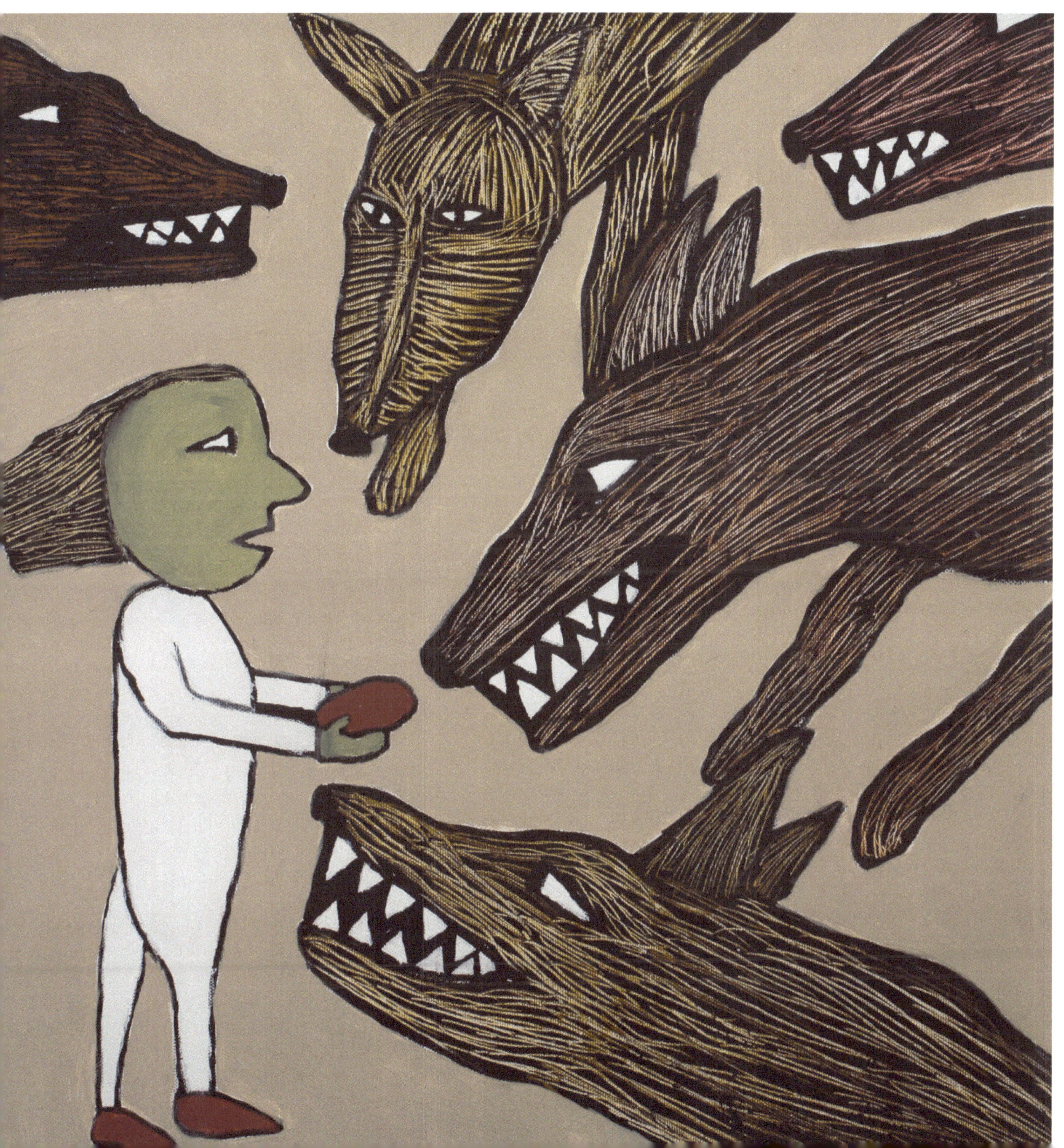

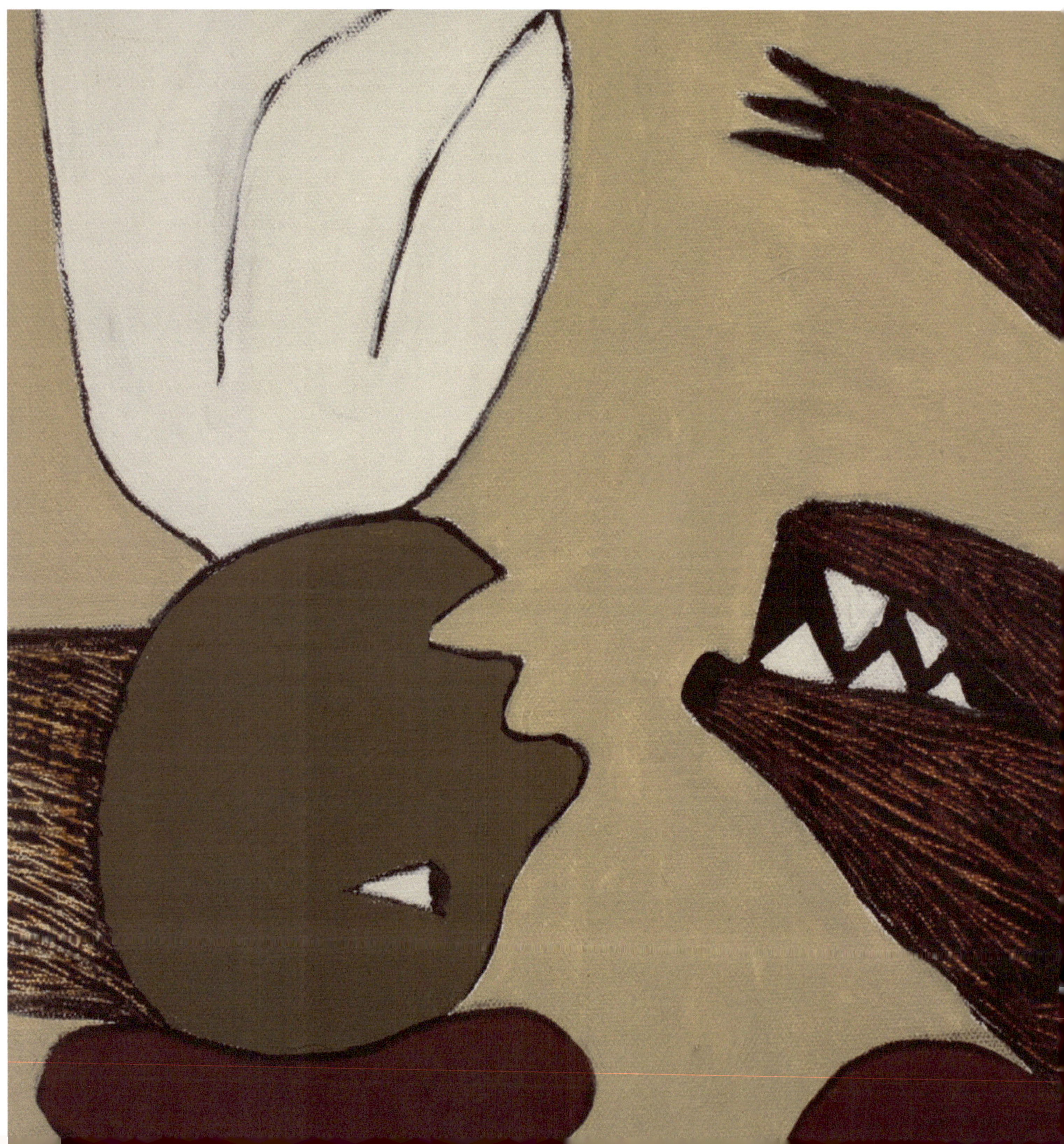

Harris gives yoga a try . . .

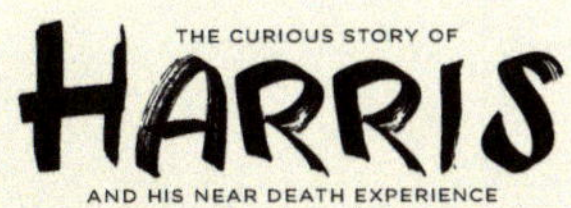

. . . and meditation.

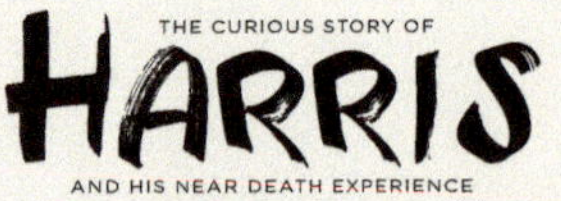

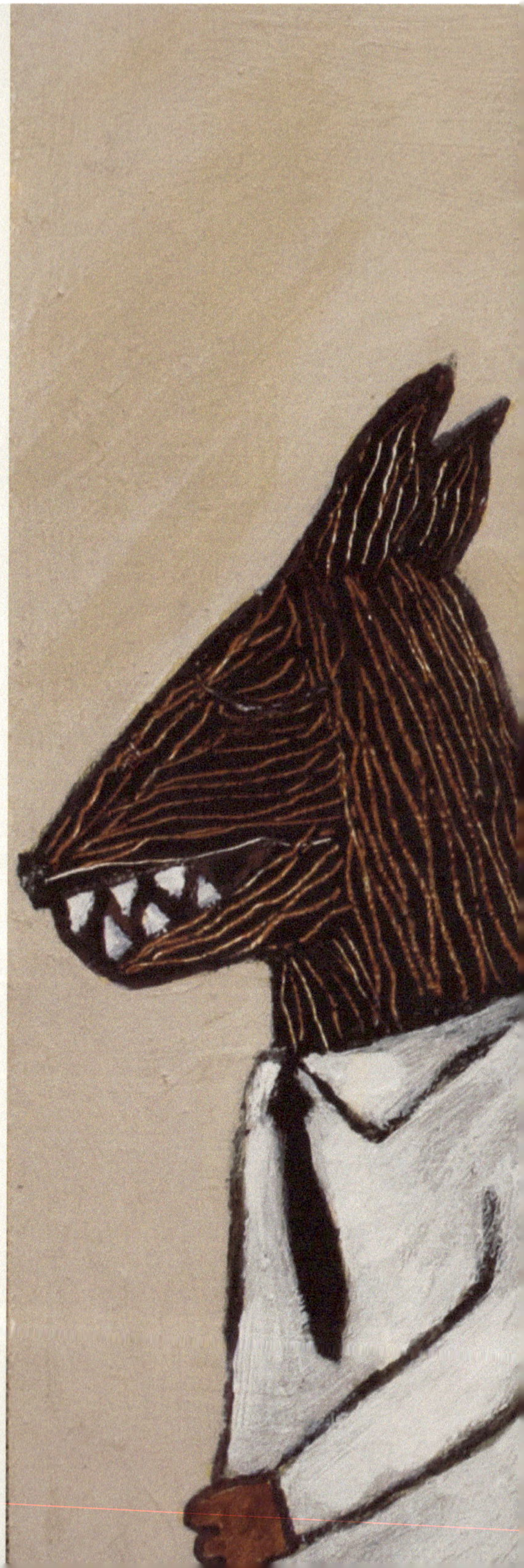

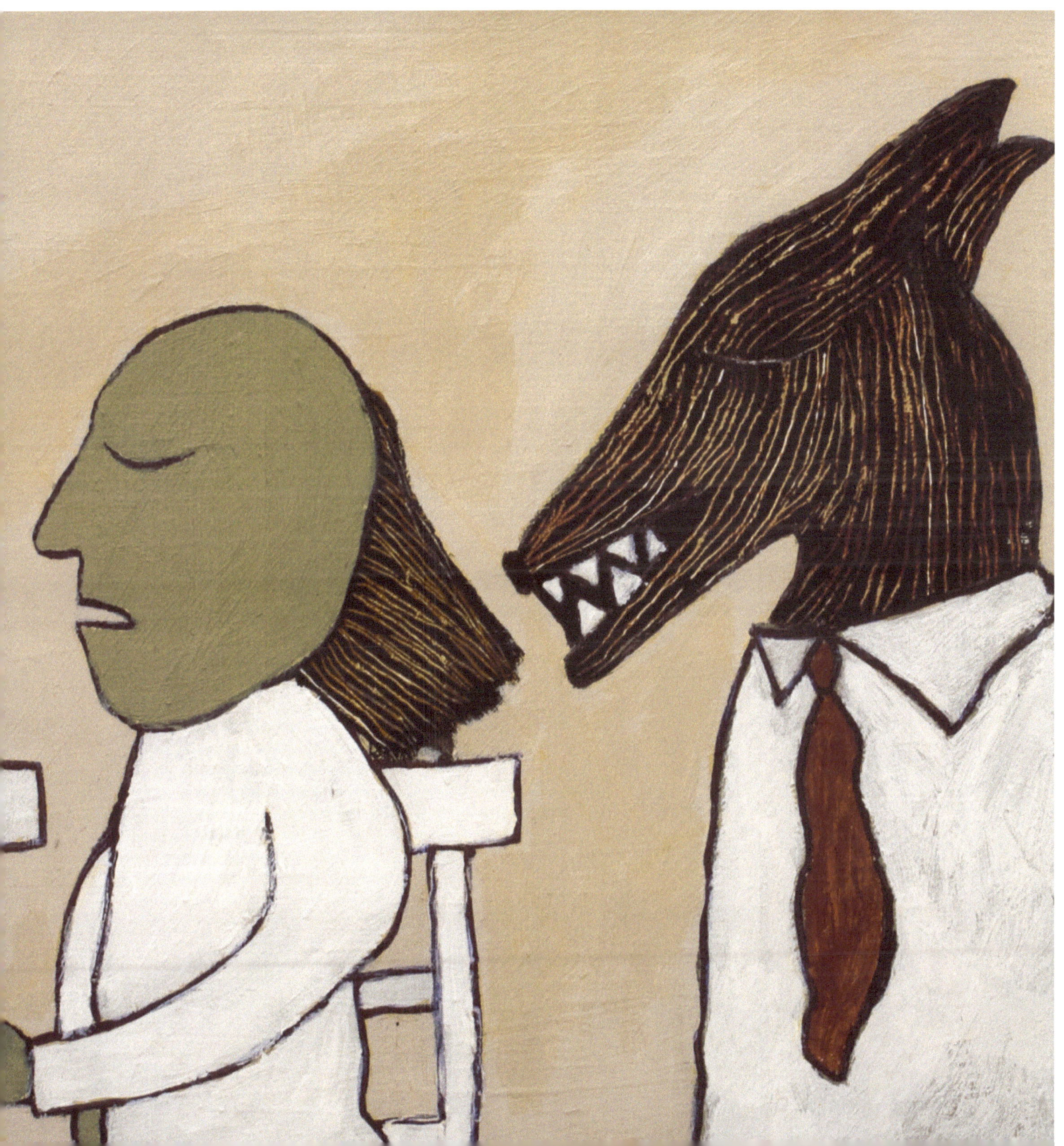

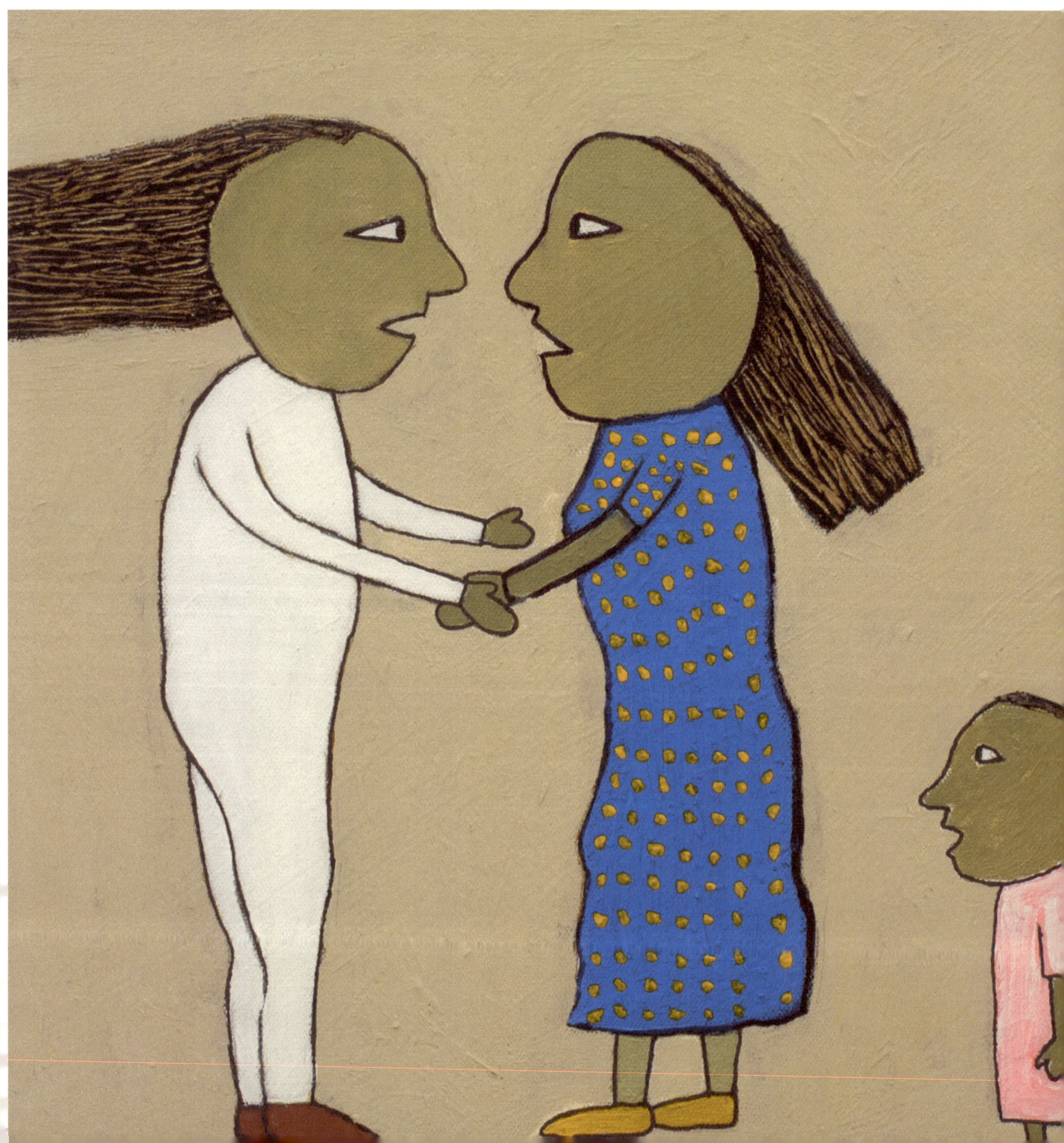

Harris tells Mrs. Harris that he has to search
for something missing in his life.

33

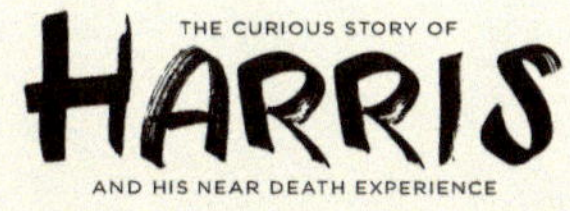

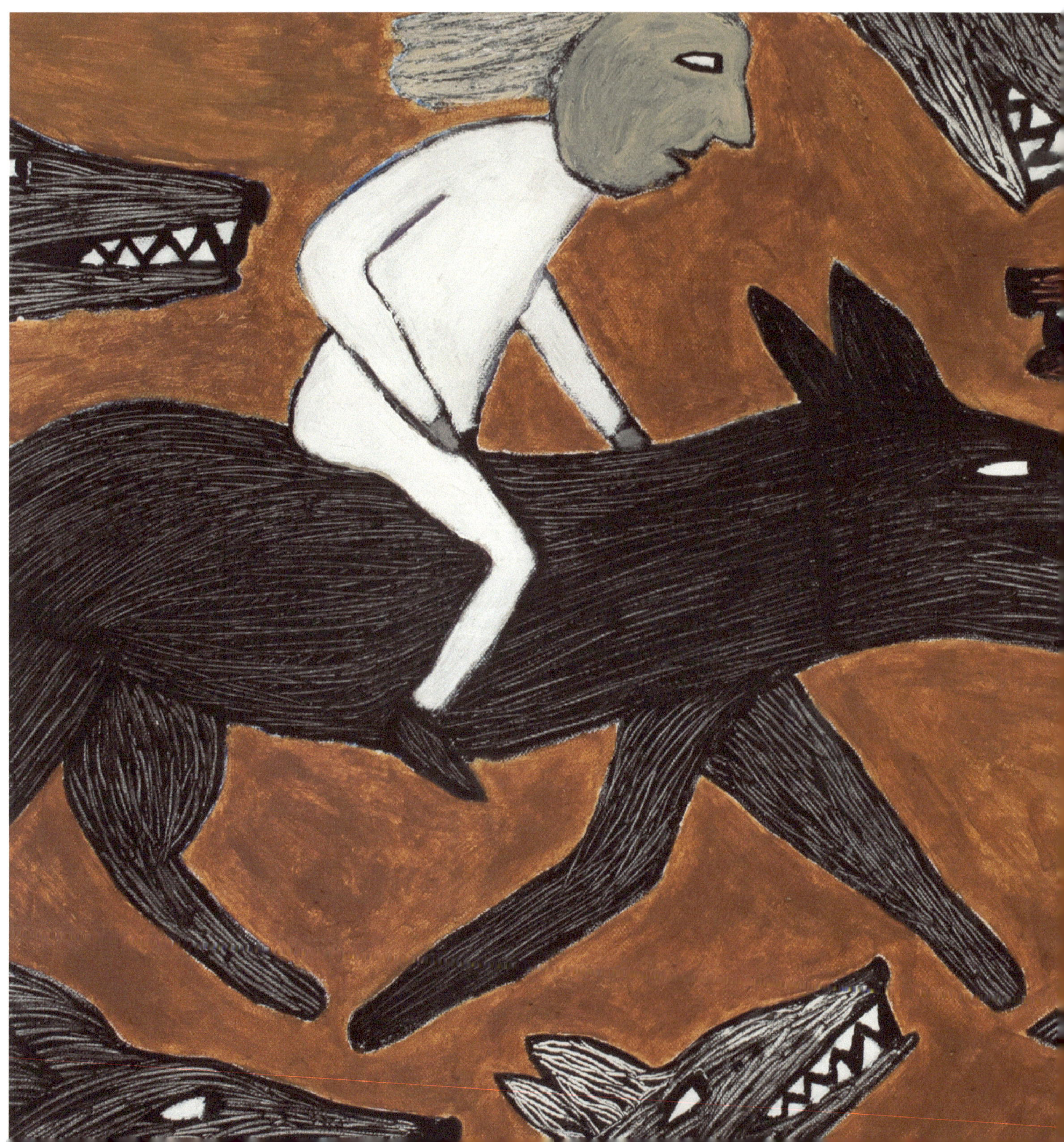

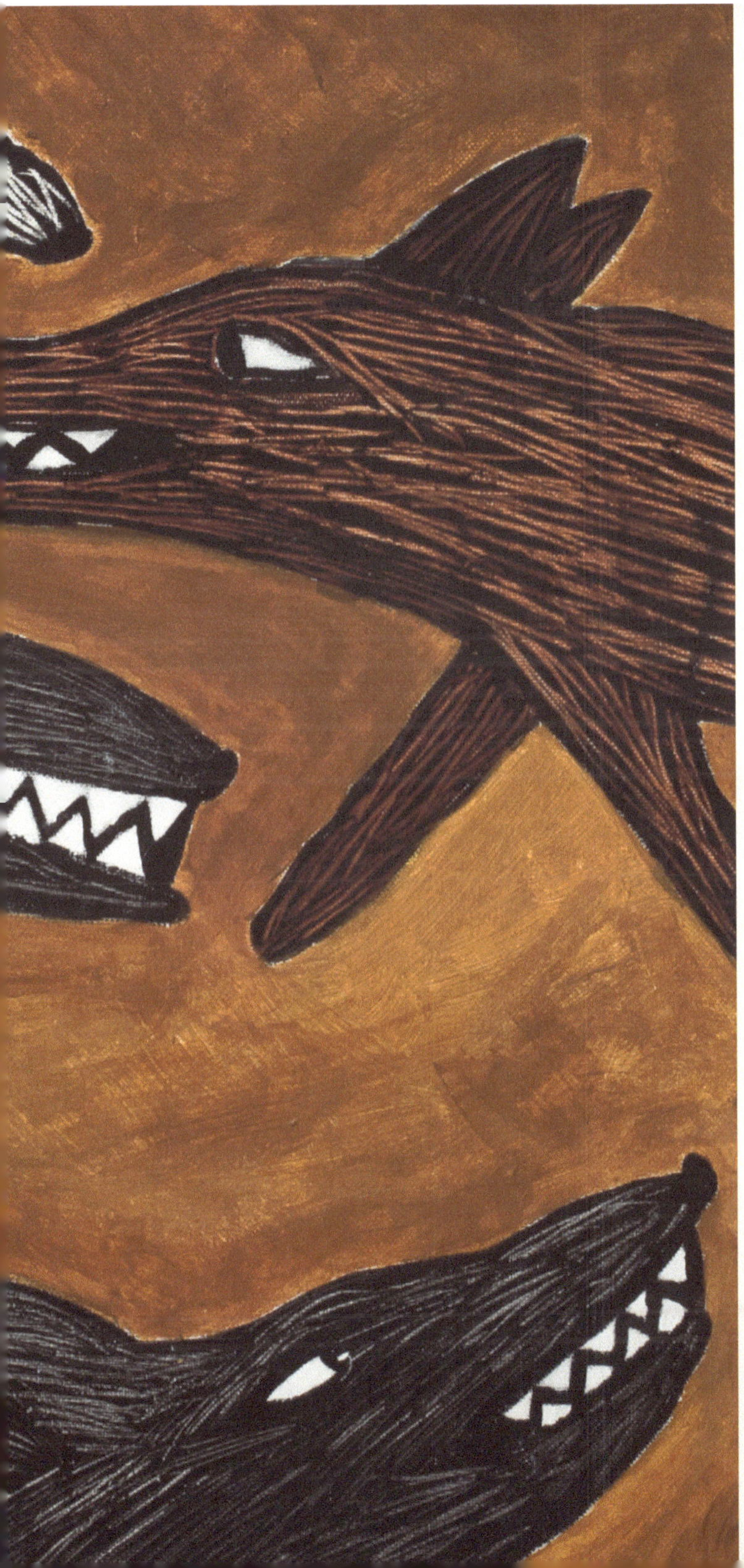

Harris rides with the wolves.

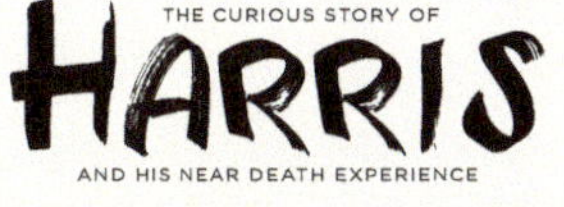

Harris goes further and further into the unknown.

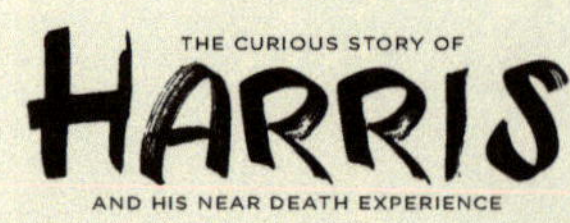

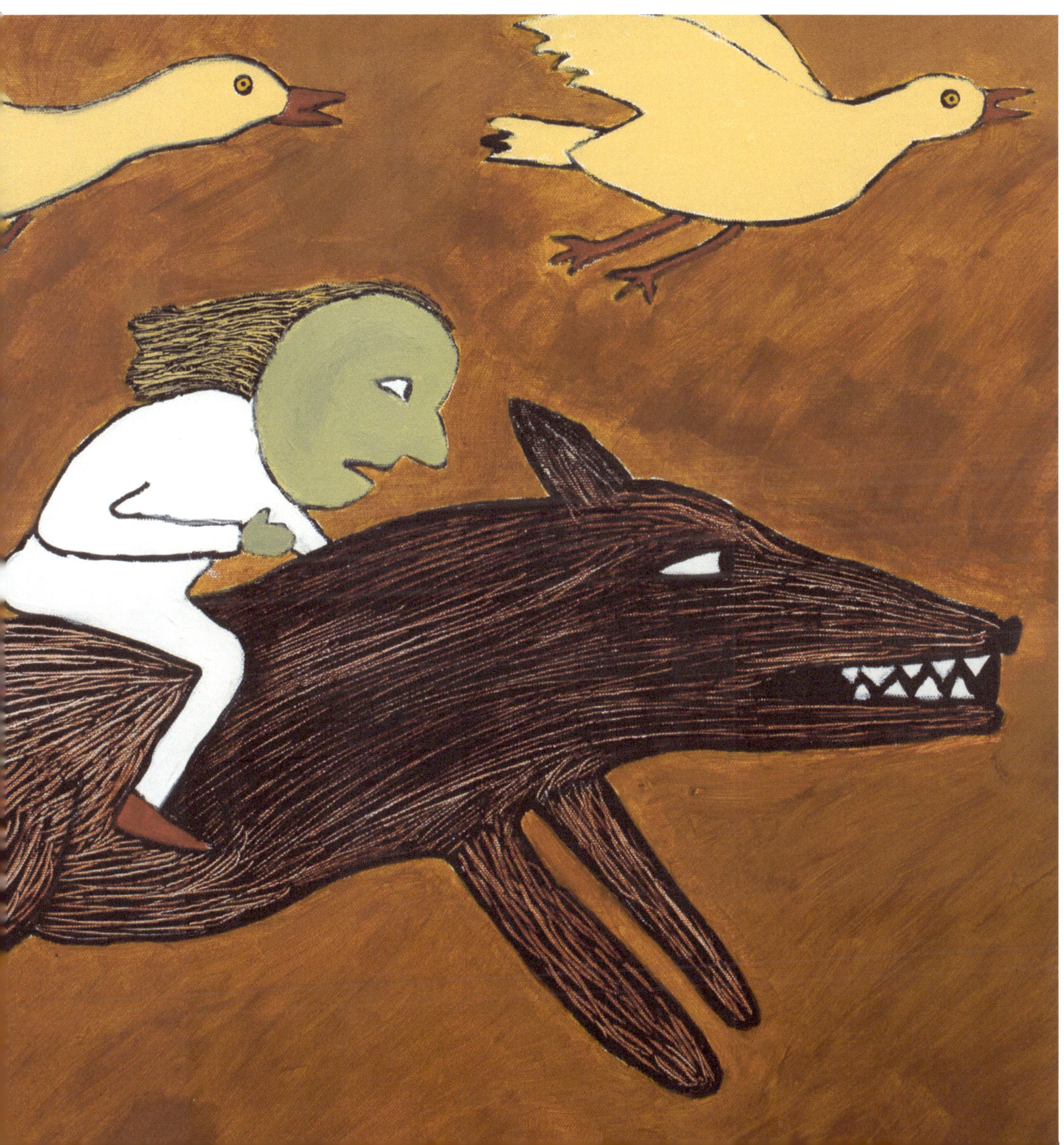

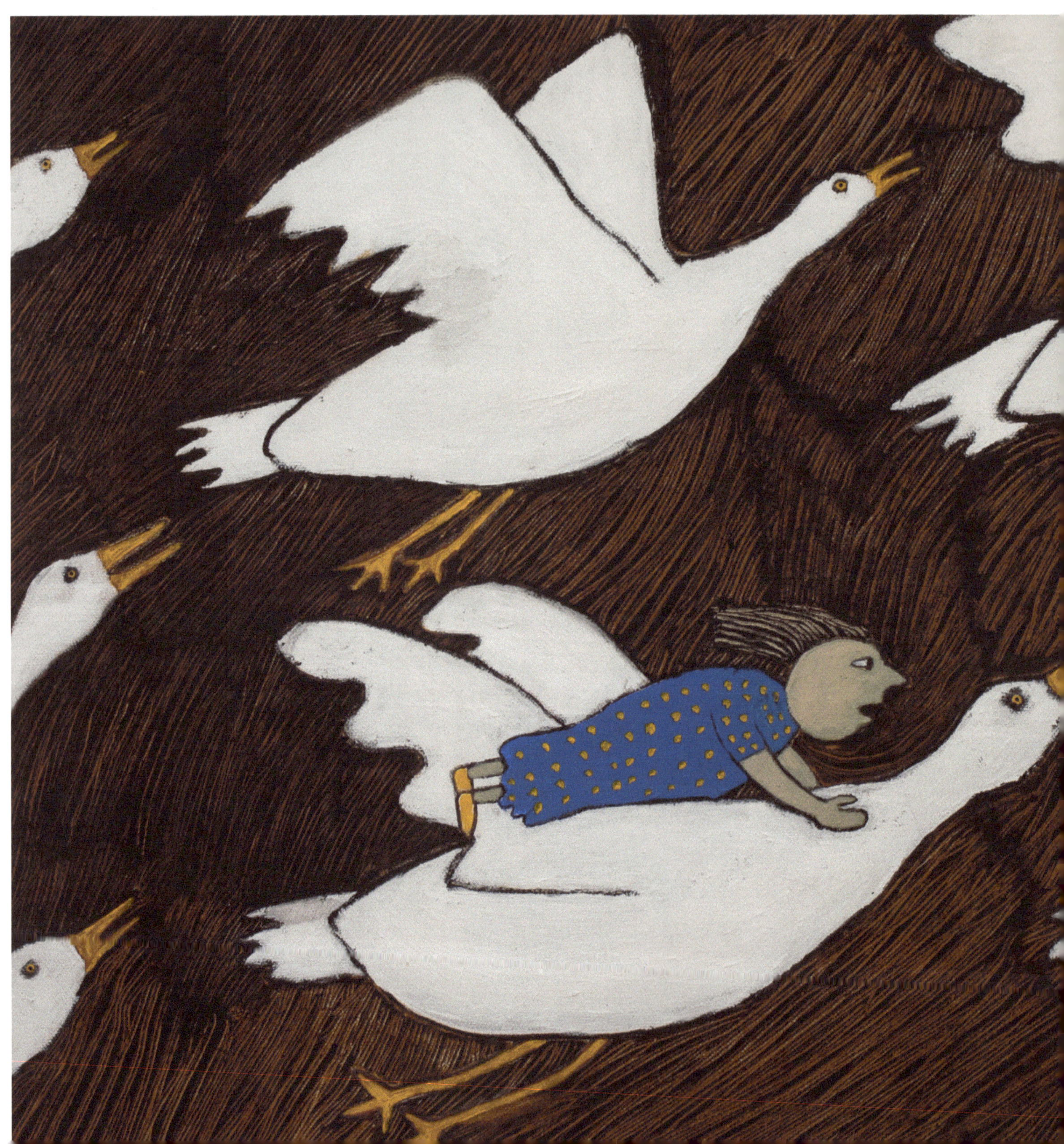

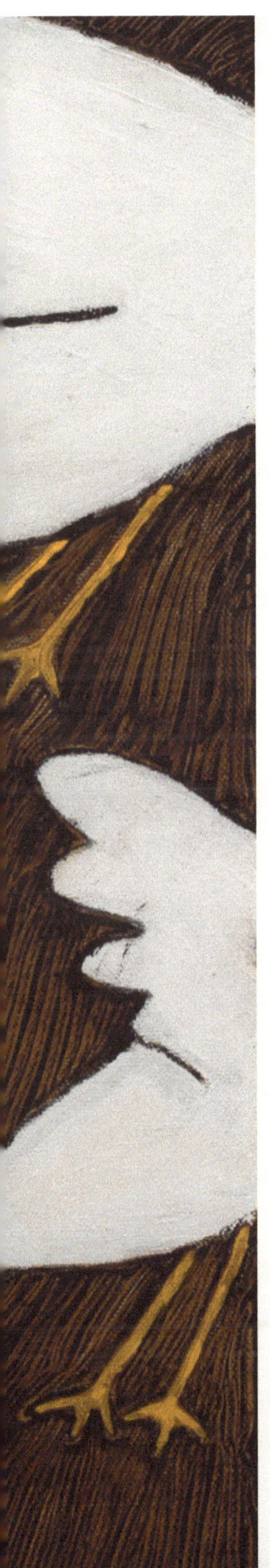

When Harris hasn't come home for several weeks
Mrs. Harris takes off to look for him.

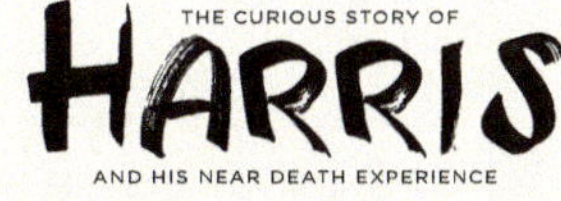

Harris is going downhill.

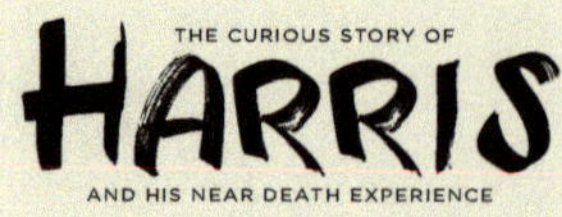

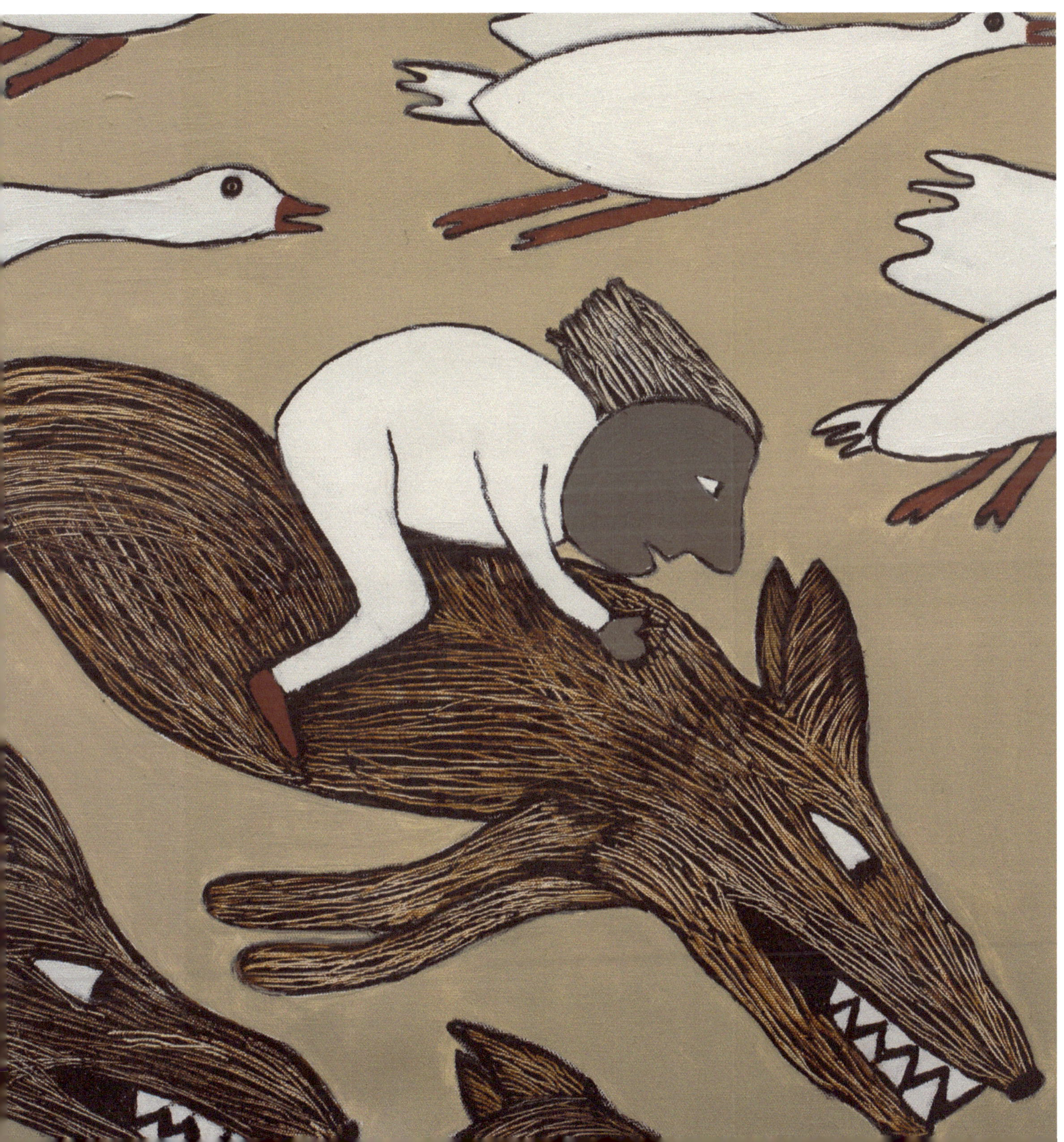

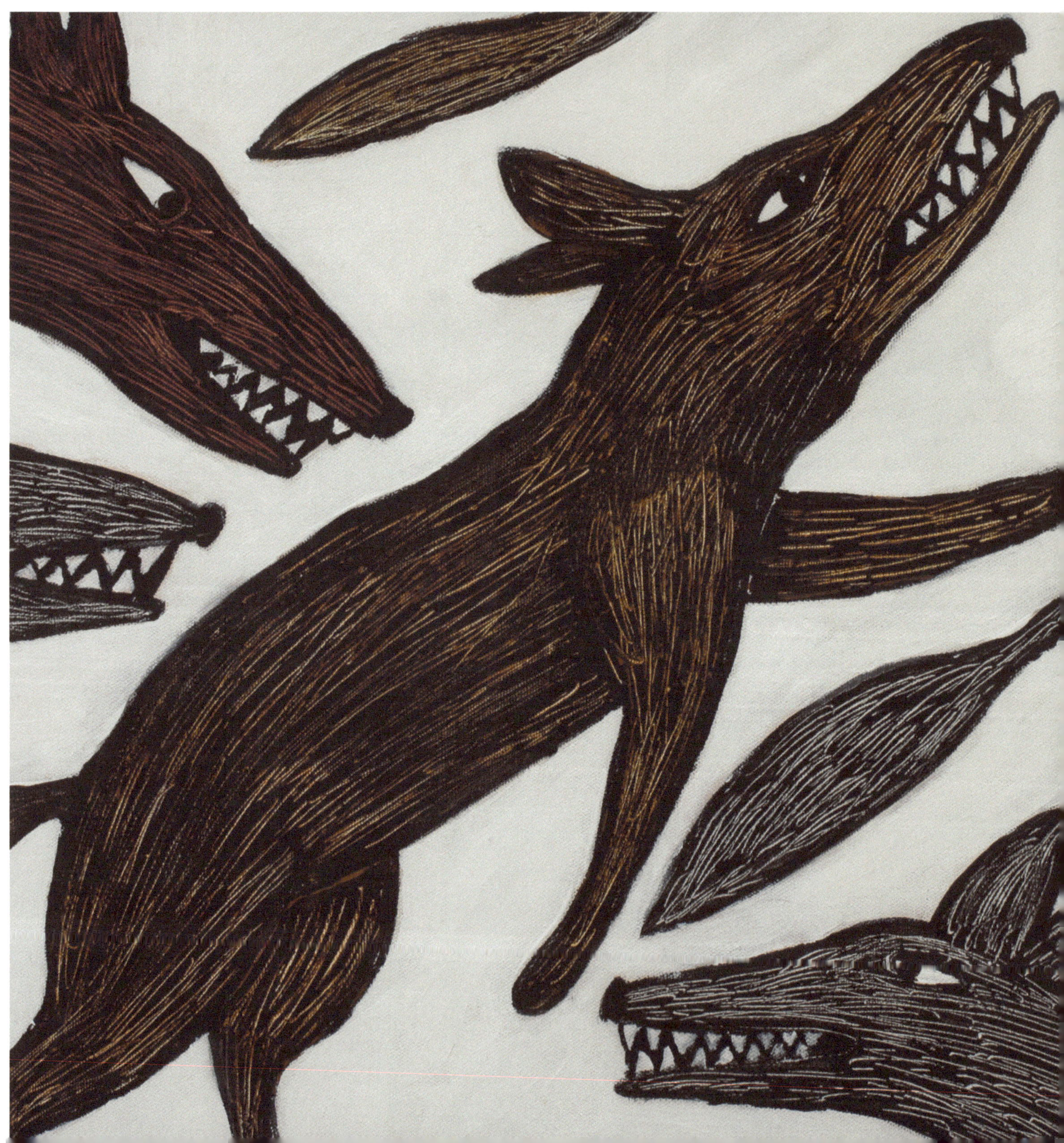

The wolves are back in his head.

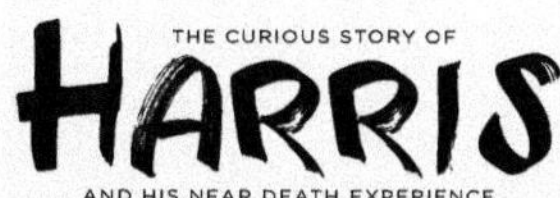

Harris decides to look for a guru . . .

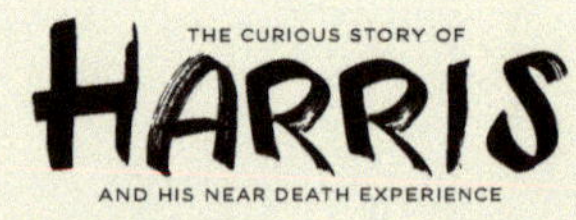

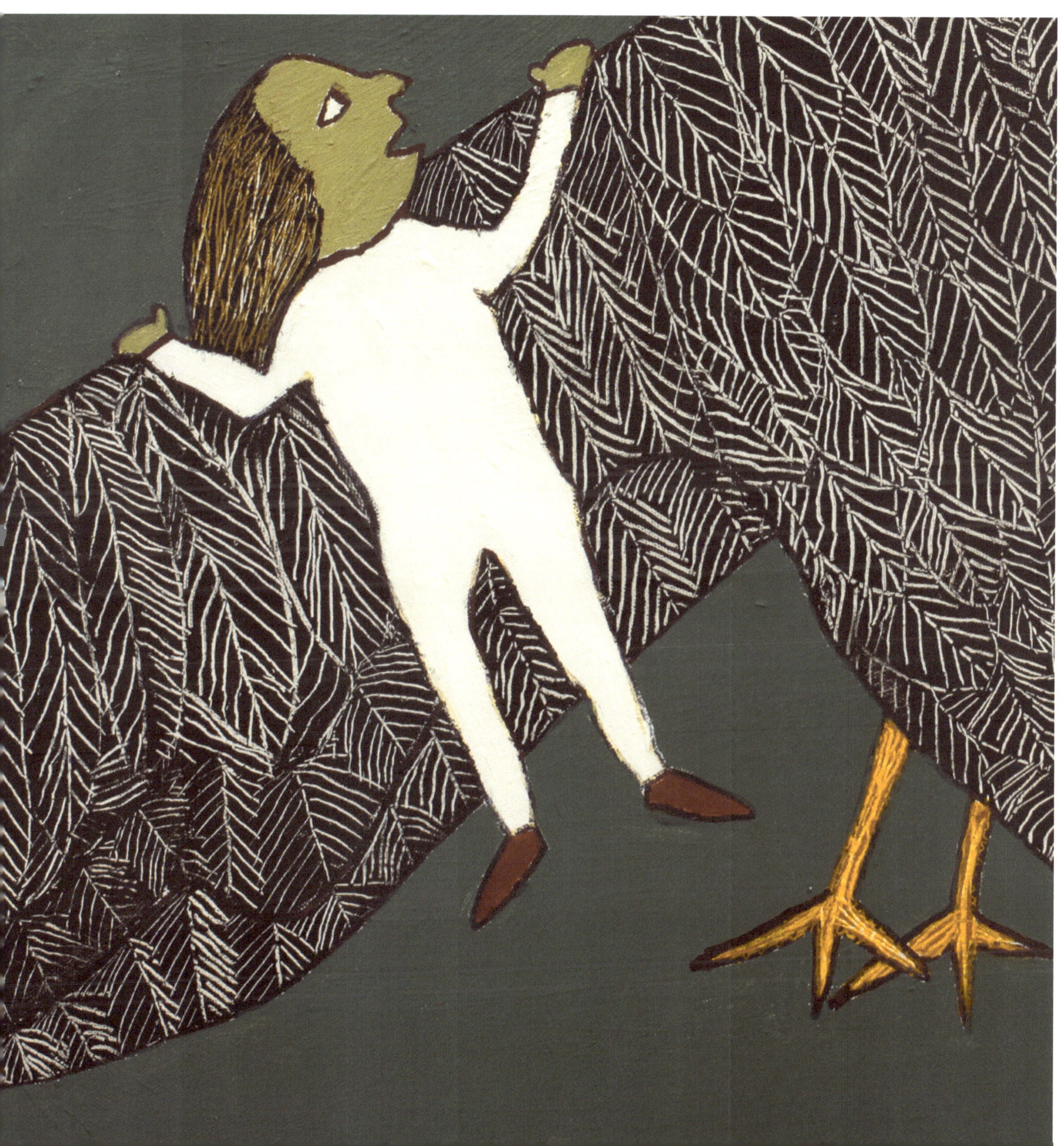

. . . but flying to India he loses his grip.

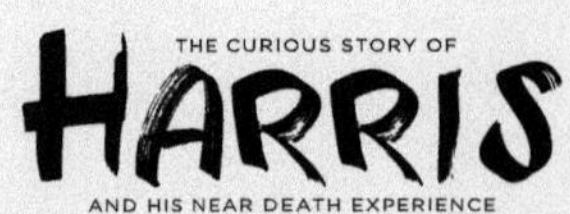

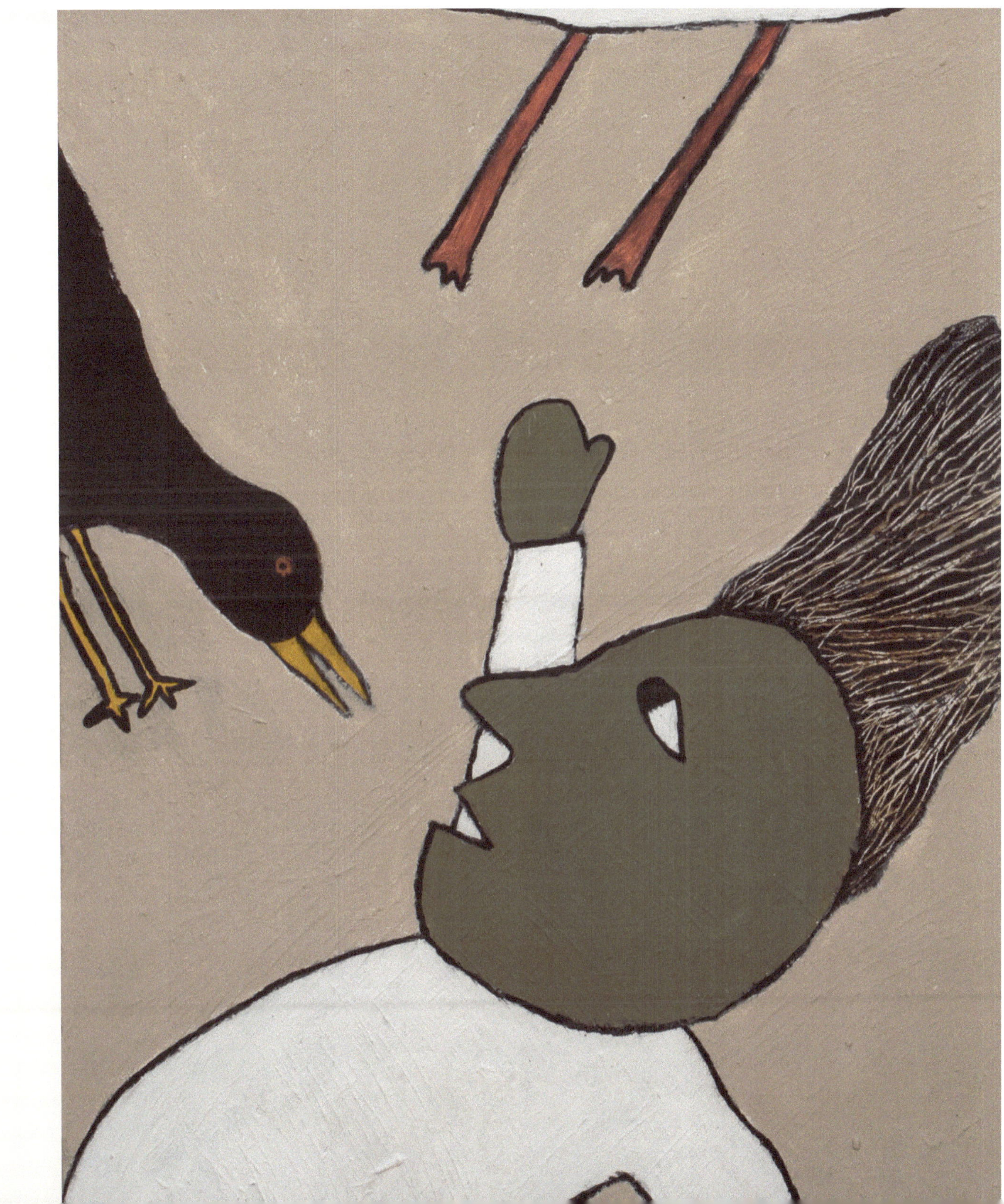

Harris feels life slipping out of his body.

48

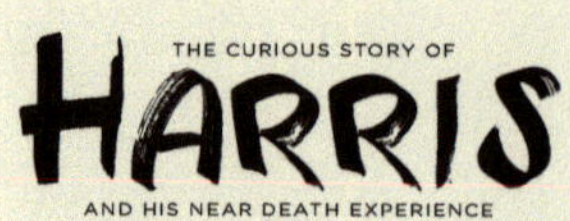

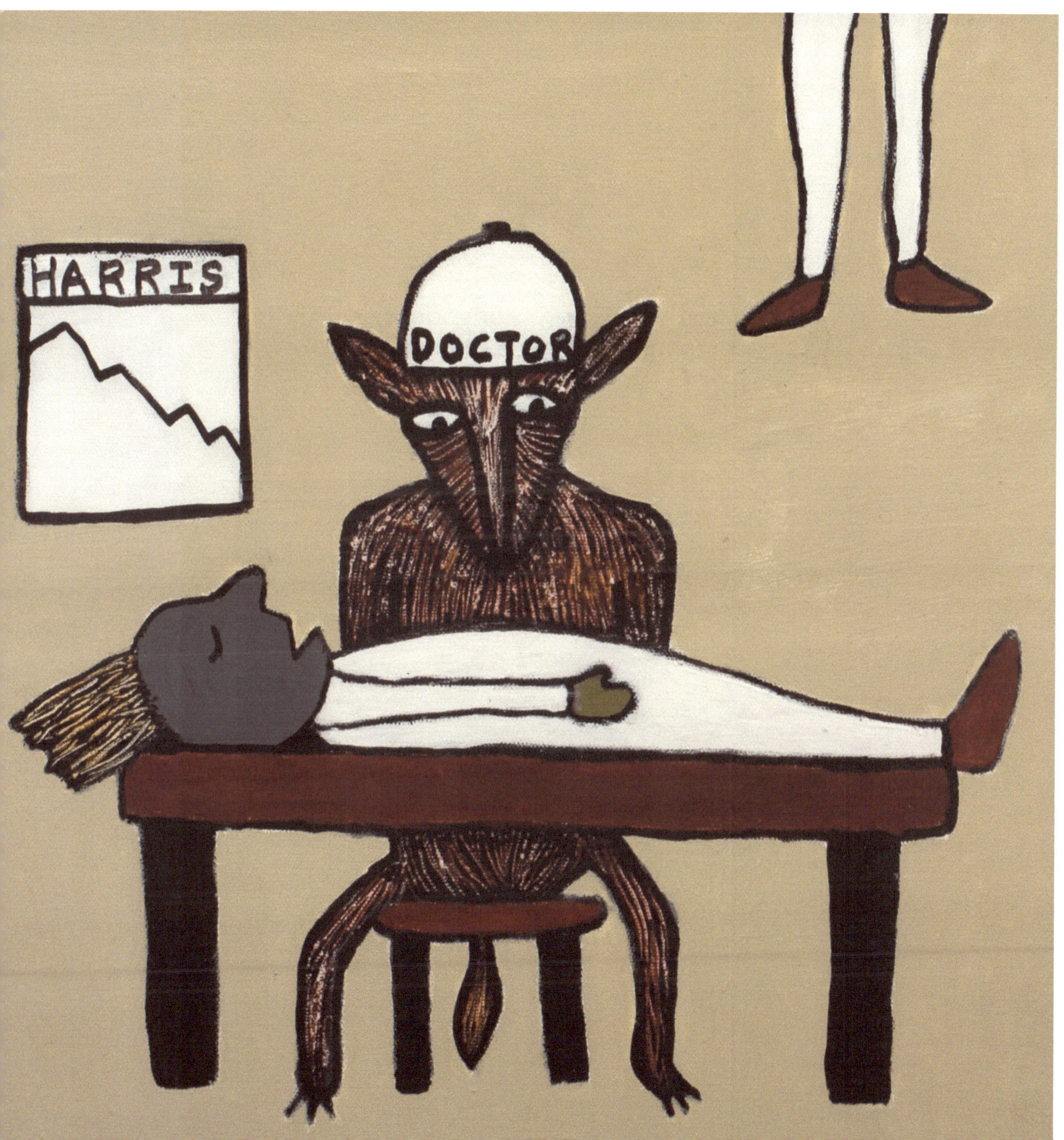
HARRIS
DOCTOR

**Uncle Howl & Aunt Pepsodent are waiting
to meet Harris at Heaven's Door.**

50

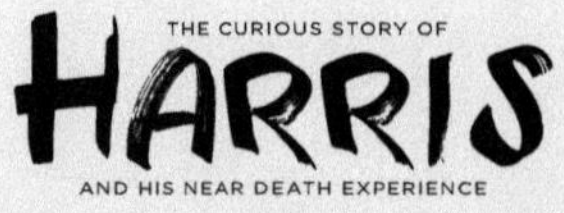

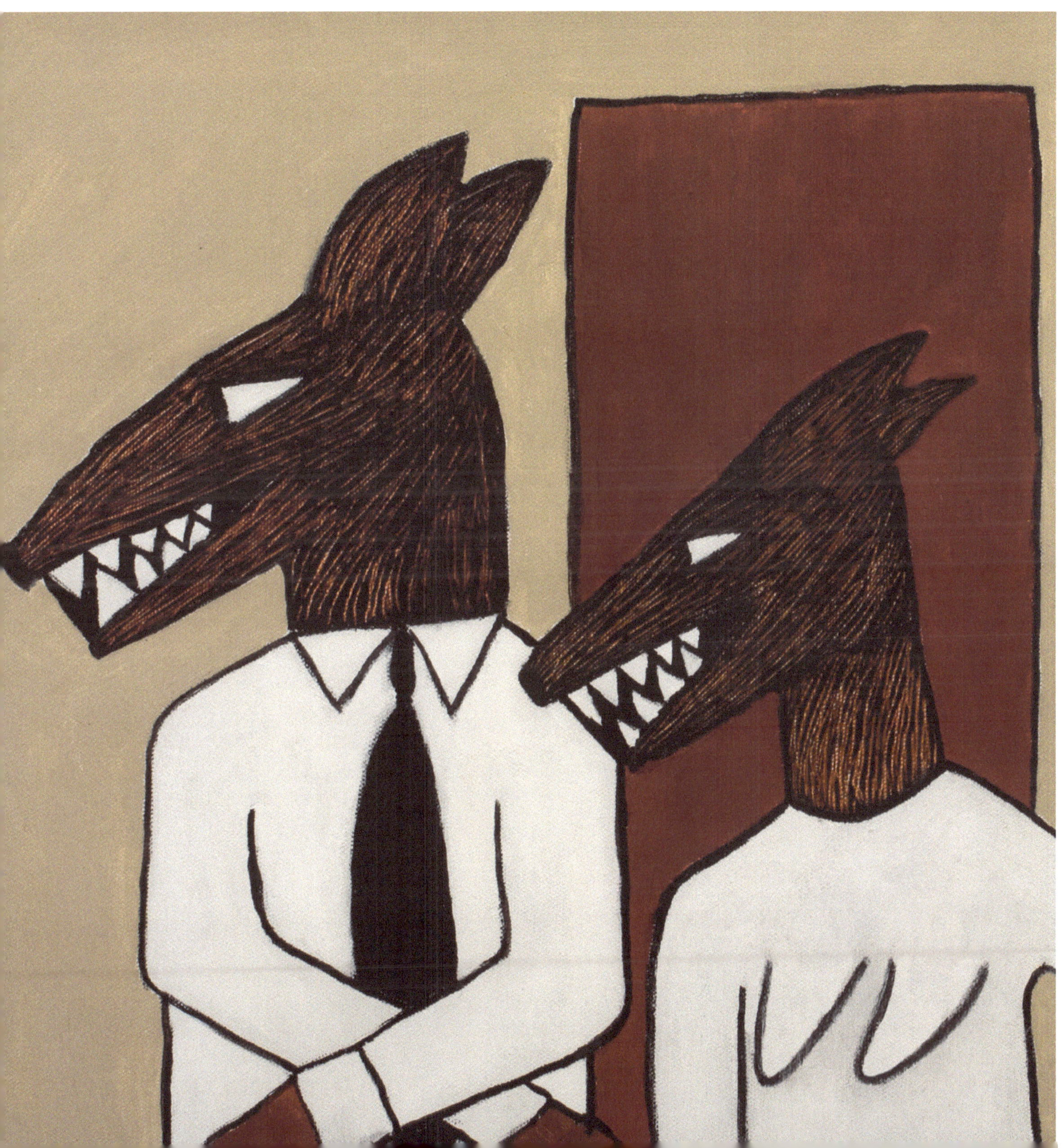

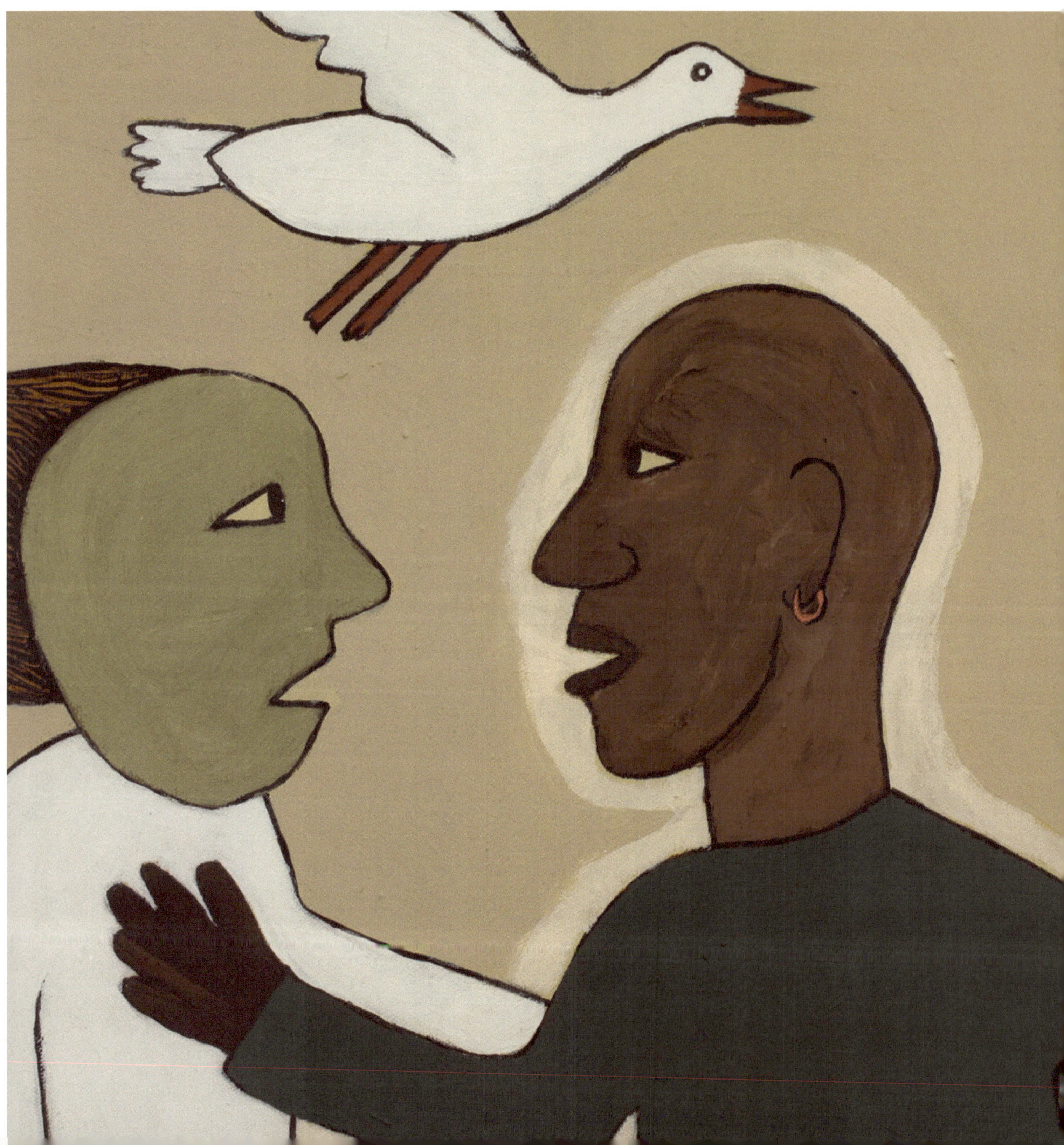

Harris meets a cool dude called Jesus who says that his Father (who seems to be the boss) reckons Harris is not ready to stay in Heaven as he has 'issues' to face on earth.

53

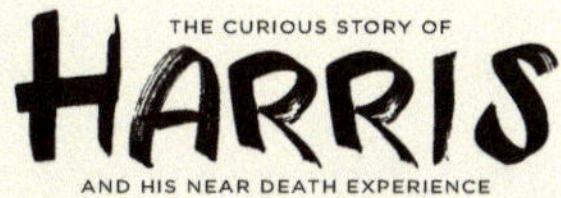

Harris races home.

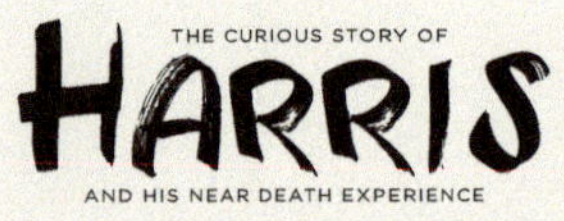

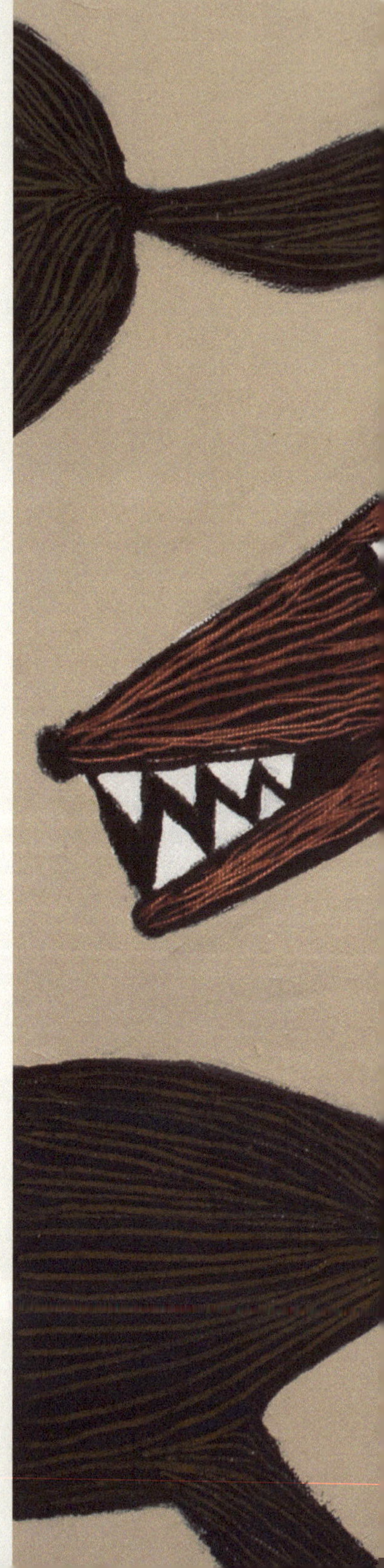

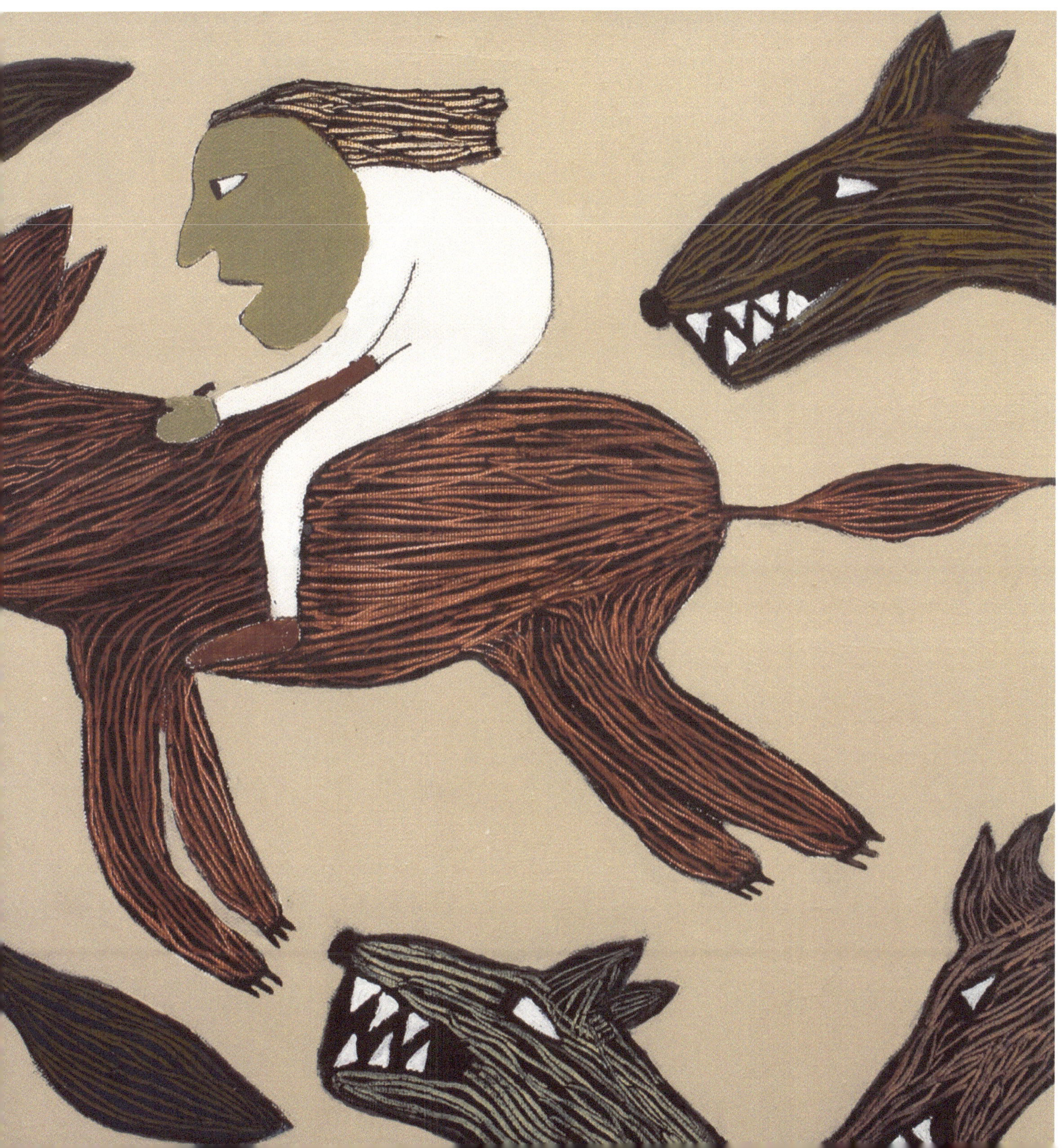

Mrs. Harris rushes to meet him.

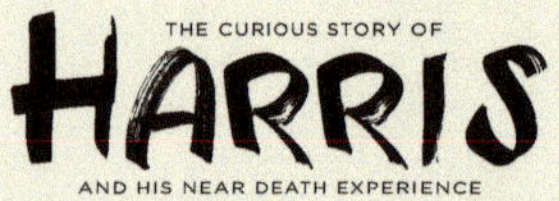

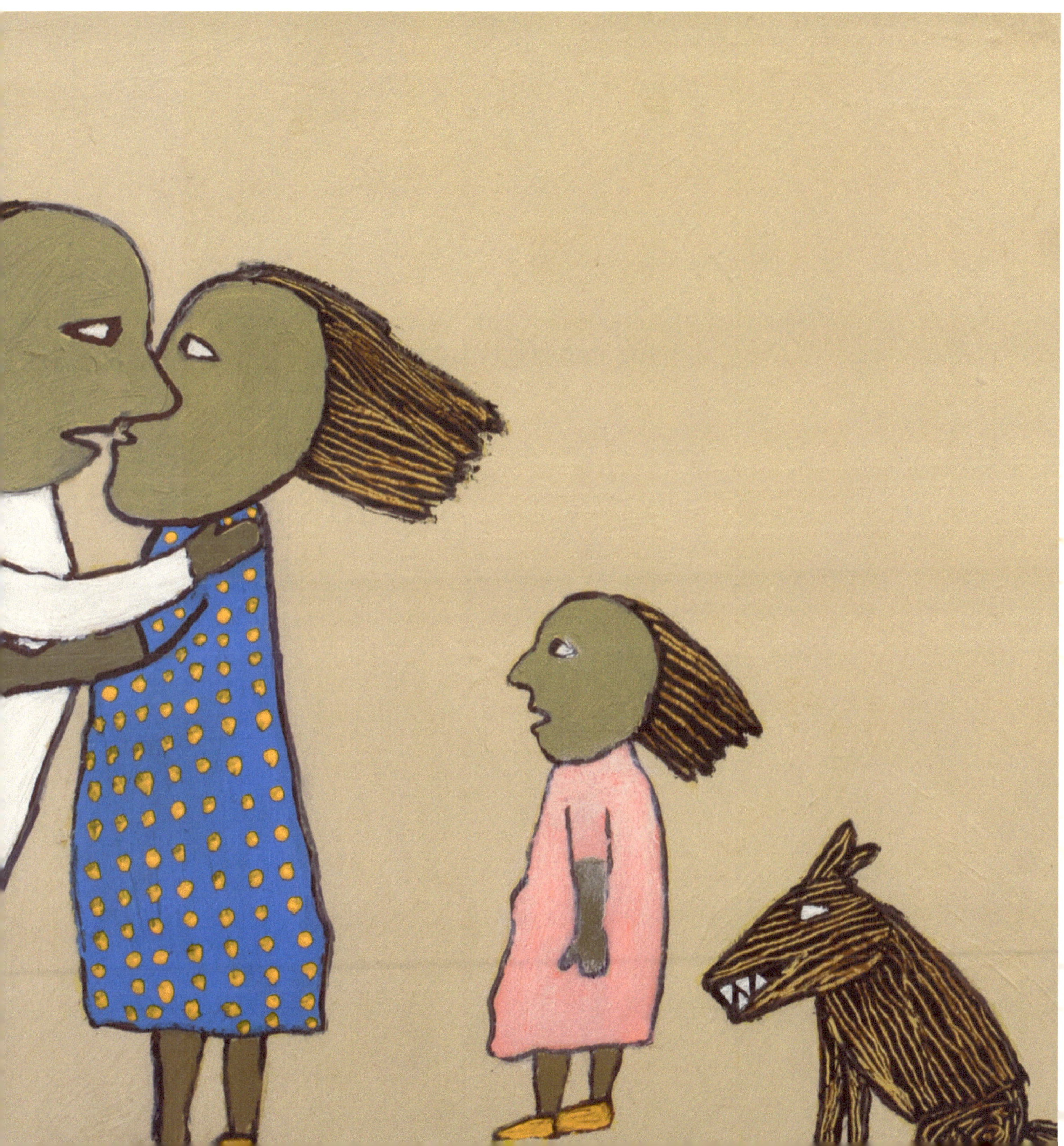

Harris tells Mrs. Harris that he never could find
anything missing from his life.

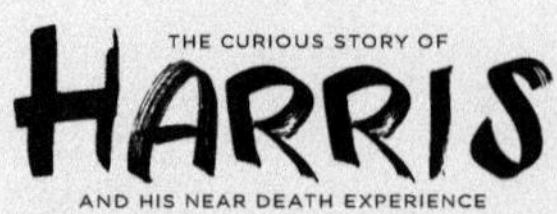

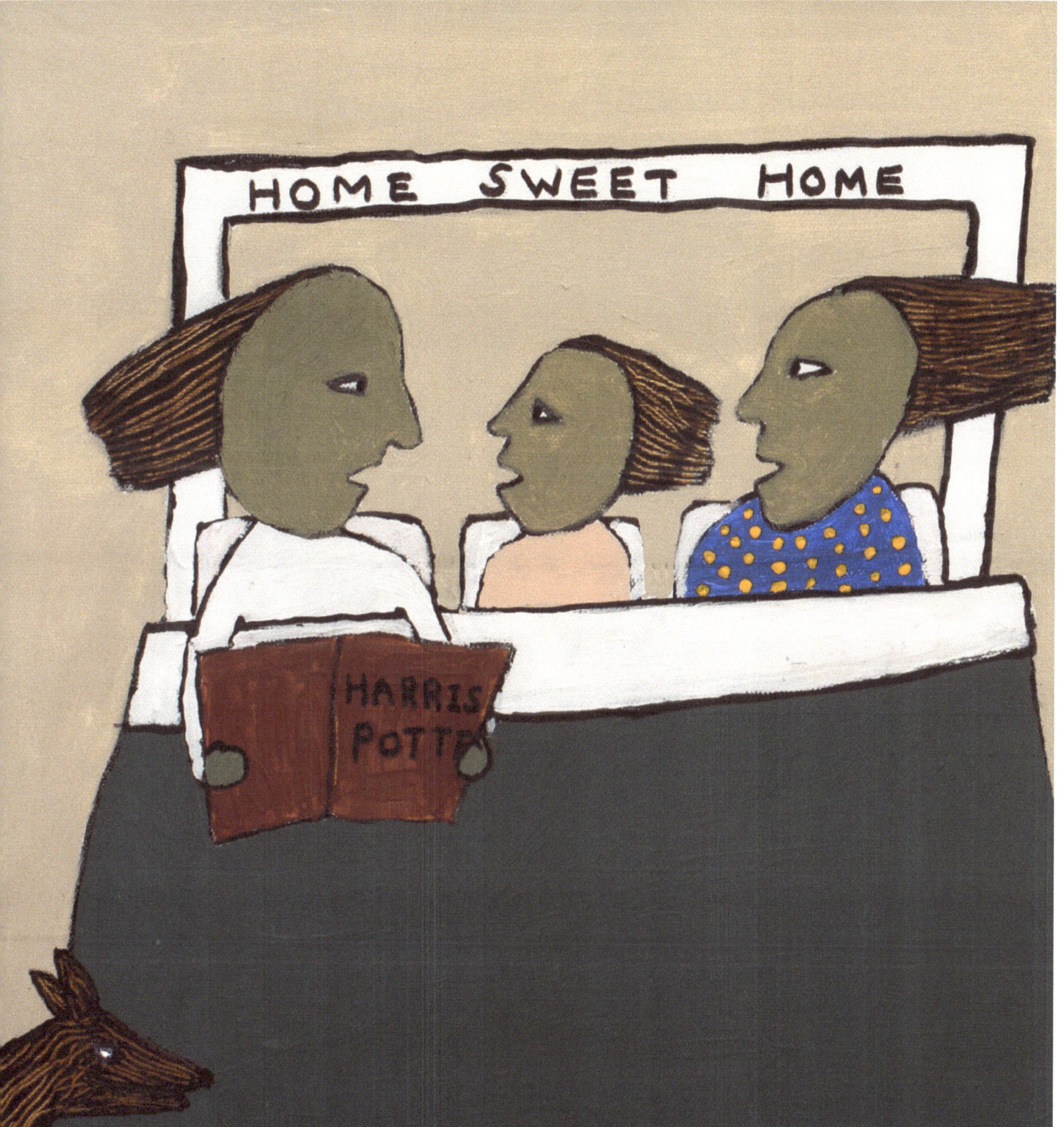
HOME SWEET HOME
HARRIS POTTE

also by **Nicholas Williamson**

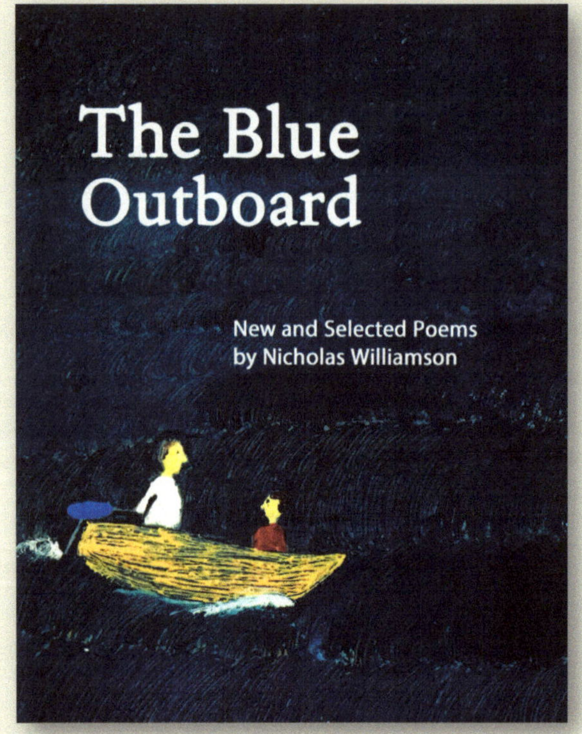

About the Author

Nicholas Williamson lives in Christchurch, New Zealand. His first book of poems, **The Whole Forest** (2001), was published by Sudden Valley Press. **'Broken Light'**, a poem from that collection was selected for Best New Zealand Poems 2001. In 2005 his poem **'Learning a Language'** won the New Zealand Poetry Society's International Poetry Competition. In 2016 a book of new and selected poems, **The Blue Outboard**, was published by Black Doris Press. Also in 2016, he began developing a series of whimsical paintings which became the curious story of Harris.

Acknowledgments

My deepest gratitude and appreciation to the following friends and colleagues without whose thoughts, insights, inspiration and expertise this book would not have been possible.

Angus McNaughton - for photographing my artwork.

Tim Gilman - for his encouragement and help.

Michael Springer & **Helene Smith** - for providing critical comment on the paintings.

let the adventure continue . . .

Yacob *&* Tomás